Sevenoaks:

THE GREAT WAR

&

ITS LEGACY

By the same author:

Sevenoaks War Memorial: The Men Remembered

Sevenoaks:

THE GREAT WAR

&

ITS LEGACY

MATTHEW BALL

Best wishes,

Matt.

Silver Pines Press

ISBN 978-0-9572631-2-3

Printed and bound in the UK by
Berforts South West Ltd
Enterprise House,B52 Wrest Park, Silsoe,
Bedfordshire MK45 4HS

Typeset in 10pt on 13pt Minion Pro

First published in the UK in 2018 by

Silver Pines Press
2 Pinewood Avenue, Sevenoaks, Kent, TN14 5AF

CONTENTS

For Ian Walker

&

Kenneth Charles Taylor
1935 - 2018

ACKNOWLEDGEMENTS

I am grateful to all who contributed to and otherwise supported the writing of this book. Above all, it would not have been possible without the generosity of those who shared their family stories, photos, diaries and memoirs of this period. In particular, I am grateful to Jane Andrews, the late Jane Ashmore, Sheila Bell, Denis Brooker, David Checkley, Jane Churchill, Norman and Julia Copper, Keith Davey, Julie Frenette, David Gillow, Peter Gillow, Keith Gordon, Martin Gordon, the estate of the late Freda Hilder, Mary and Carol Horncastle, Angela Hudson, Ingleby Jefferson, the Mansfield family, Tim Marshall, Tim Pearce, Barbara and Keith Reddy, Edward Rogers, Jane Taylor, the late Mollie Tester, David Terry, Valerie Tuttle, Adrian Whyntie, and the late Philip Wren. I hope I have done justice to the material that they were so kind to share.

Thanks also to Linda Larter MBE, Town Clerk of Sevenoaks Town Council, and the Council itself, for the award of a grant toward the costs of this book. My thanks to Robert Illingworth, Community History Officer, Kent County Council Libraries, Registration & Archives, Sally Robinson, archivist at Sevenoaks School, Angela Prior-Wandesforde of Knole (National Trust), Steve Finnis of The Queen's Own Royal West Kent Regiment Museum and Peter Donnelly, Curator, Kings Own Royal Regiment Museum (*kingsownmuseum.com*).

Social historian, Emma Muscat, generously allowed me to use her images of the Forster memorial in the church of St Katherine, Exbury.

Alice Busvine, John Hamblin, Linda Larter, Simon Last, Pam Mills, Bob Ogley, and John Wood all read a draft copy of this book and were encouraging at that anxious hour before publication. My thanks to Sebastian Stead for his excellent photography of the Commonwealth War Graves at Greatness Cemetery. Steph Harrison has been an enthusiastic champion of this book and of the town's plans to mark the centenary. Cliff Rumsey has generously driven the 'Sevenoaks Pals' around the battlefields of France, visiting the graves of many of the Sevenoaks fallen. My thanks to James Skinner of Silver Pines Press for bringing four years of research to life so sympathetically.

This book was researched and written around my day job. James Seabrooke has allowed me the flexibility to ensure that I can do both and been a generous friend and colleague throughout.

My friend, Ian Walker, has been my companion in research, interpretation and enjoyment of our common interest in the First World War for the last five years. I am grateful for his enthusiasm, guidance, and expertise. He also read early drafts and encouraged my research. In particular, the section on the hidden casualties of the war is inspired by his examination of the theme. I am pleased to dedicate this book to him in thanks.

An accident in 2017 at least afforded me five weeks of convalescence and the time to read every edition of the *Sevenoaks Chronicle* and *Kent Messenger* from 1914 – 1922. Scott Craddock looked after me, conveyed me to the Accident and Emergency of Cheltenham Hospital, and eventually worked out how to push the wheelchair in the right direction. I hope he knows how grateful I am. My parents and brother, Stuart, helped me recover, aided by my aunts, Marion and Valerie, who appeared with a welcome amount of cake and trifle. My auntie Pat didn't appear with cake but, as a boy, with her library of books on the Kings and Queens of England, she helped inspire and shared my love of history. Her husband, my uncle Ken, was an important part of my childhood and, most of all, made me laugh. He died as this book was being prepared for publication and shares the dedication. My aunt, Daphne, and uncles, Brian and John, have also shared my love of history and always been encouraging.

Finally, my nephew, Jacob Southway Neil, was born to Stuart and Katie on New Year's Eve morning 2017. Nearly one hundred years after his death on 13th October 1918, the life of Private Frederick Southway, 52435 1st Battalion Worcestershire Regiment, is still recalled in our family. Frederick was a close friend of my late grandfather, Lionel, who gave my father the same middle name. Nearly a century on, we remember still.

~

A NOTE ON SOURCES

I have used a wide range of available sources in the research and writing of this book.

Anyone wishing to trace their military ancestors or their wider family tree or even a War Memorial or Roll of Honour, should consider using one of the subscription based websites, such as *ancestry.co.uk* and *findmypast.co.uk*. Both of these sites are excellent resources for the annual censuses, births, marriages and deaths. They also hold military service papers and other records relating to ordinary servicemen.

The records of officers killed during the war, where they survive, are held at the National Archives at Kew. The type of material held in them varies, but they can be a treasure trove of information.

The records of the Commonwealth War Graves Commission, available online at *cwgc.org* are a valuable source and a guide to where each man is buried or remembered.

The local papers of the time, the *Sevenoaks Chronicle*, *Kent Messenger*, and *Kent & Sussex Courier* are excellent sources of information on all aspects of the war. The *Chronicle* is available to view at Sevenoaks Library on microfiche and the *Messenger* is available online via the Kent Library Service. The *Chronicle* and the *Courier* are also available online via the British Newspaper Archive at *britishnewspaperarchive.co.uk.*

The record cards of many VAD nurses are available via the British Red Cross at *vad.redcross.org.uk*

For anyone wishing to learn more about the war in general, *longlongtrail.co.uk* contains detailed information on all aspects of the conflict. The Great War Forum *1914-1918invisionzone.com* allows members to post queries and discuss research with likeminded individuals.

The Western Front Association, the North West Kent branch of which meets on the last Thursday of most months at Petts Wood, near Sevenoaks, is an excellent organisation, devoted to the study of the Great War. The WFA can be found online at *westernfrontassociation.com.*

The Kent History and Library Centre, with its knowledgeable and helpful staff, holds much material of interesting, including records of the Military Tribunals in the county. The Museum of the Queen's Own (Royal West Kent Regiment) is also based at Maidstone.

The North West Kent Family History Association is also an invaluable source of information and advice and can be found at ***nwkfhs.org.uk.***

Of course, any mistakes, either factual or of interpretation, are my own. Every attempt has been made to acknowledge and respect copyright of all materials used. Any errors or omissions will be corrected when possible.

~

INTRODUCTION

It was clear from the research involved in my first book *'Sevenoaks War Memorial: The Men Remembered',* that there were other stories of the period which should be told. Our town War Memorial at the Vine is almost the sole public reminder of how the Great War affected the people of Sevenoaks. But it only symbolises part of the story. When the memorial was unveiled in 1920, it was estimated that approximately 1200 townsmen had served in the armed forces. More had come from the neighbouring villages. These stories, of the men who fought and returned, many physically and mentally scarred, also deserve to be told. As do the stories of those who chose not to fight, who stood up for their beliefs as Conscientious Objectors, and did so against a background of patriotic fervour. I also wanted to explore the wartime experiences of the women of Sevenoaks.

At the outbreak of war, Sevenoaks was a quiet market town, which had benefitted from the arrival of the railway, first at Bat and Ball, and then at Tubs Hill stations. The town was swiftly transformed by war. Belgian refugees began to arrive within weeks of August 1914, followed by the first wounded men. Thousands of soldiers arrived in the town, many to be billeted in private homes. Others were accommodated in tents in Knole Park and elsewhere. Daily life was, suddenly, very different. Lancashire accents mingled with Belgian ones. Wounded and disabled men appeared in the streets. Men disappeared from homes, shops, and business, as they volunteered to enlist in the battalions of Lord Kitchener's New Army – 'Kitchener's Mob'. Pub hours were curtailed, curfews were proposed, there were fewer goods in the shops, fundraising began for numerous good causes. There were new concerns, such as the threat from the air, as Zeppelins passed over Sevenoaks and the blackout required rendered the town in darkness.

Sevenoaks casualties largely followed the national pattern. The 10 killed in 1914 were mostly regular soldiers, those who were already serving in the army or who had been swiftly recalled from the Reserve. The early volunteers to Kitchener's Army were still in training. In 1915, 29 men were killed, including soldiers who were at Gallipoli. 1916, which saw the start of the battle of the Somme in the July, finished with 57 casualties. Many of these were the new recruits: boyhood pals, neighbours, colleagues, parishioners. Fewer bodies were recovered for burial.

Back home, people read the local papers to keep abreast of the progress of the war. The Roll of Honour in the *Sevenoaks Chronicle* bore witness to the heavy toll of wounded, gassed, and killed. Seventy lost their lives in 1917, 52 in the final months of the war in 1918 (a few died after the Armistice or have yet to be identified). Others would live with their wounds or die as a result of them long after the end of hostilities.

Like others throughout the country, the women of Sevenoaks, from across all classes, volunteered in different ways. They nursed, worked in munitions factories and on the land, ran canteens, fundraised, and knitted clothes for those at the Front.

I have endeavoured to present as rounded an assessment of the town during the war as possible and chosen stories that illustrate more general themes. Inevitably, this is based on available sources and involves a degree of selection. I hope that this book conveys something of how one town in Kent was affected by the conflict and how its residents coped with the many wartime challenges on the Home Front.

For me, the annual promise of remembrance is wider than a commitment simply to honour the fallen. It is about recalling all affected by the first global conflict and ensuring that their stories are not forgotten.

We Will Remember Them.

Matthew Ball

Sevenoaks, June 2018

More information can be found online at *sevenoaksww1.org* or on twitter *@7oaksww1*

email. matt@sevenoaksww1.org

~

Part One

AT WAR

Patriotic Fervour

For some, war between England and Germany had seemed inevitable. To Earl Stanhope, owner of Chevening House and estate just west of Sevenoaks, it was obvious. After he left the army in 1908, Stanhope devoted time and energy to the National Service League, urging support for the League's proposal for compulsory military service for home defence. According to his own memoirs, Stanhope spoke in the House of Lords on 21st April 1913, to remind the Government that the country was a signatory to the 1839 treaty that guaranteed Belgium independence. This, he suggested, meant that they should consider either denouncing the treaty or be prepared to enter a continental war, should one arise. Stanhope and supporters such as J.S. Norman, headmaster of the New Beacon Preparatory School in Sevenoaks, spoke at meetings in the town highlighting the threat from Germany.

As Second in Command of the 4th Battalion The Queen's Own Royal West Kent Regiment [1] (Territorials), Stanhope arrived at Longmoor, near Aldershot, on 26th July 1914, for the annual two weeks of training. Yearly attendance at camp was a requirement of every man's service. As the Territorials marched from Aldershot to Salisbury Plain, news eventually reached them of the order for mobilisation and, despite a lack of trains, arrangements were made for the men to return home early. They finally began to depart on 4th August, the day that war was declared.

Some, like Cedric Gordon of Sevenoaks, already a young junior officer in the 1st Battalion of the North Staffordshire Regiment, believed that the conflict would be short. He wrote on 7th August, just three days after Britain had declared war, *'I shall be back home by Christmas. You just see if I'm not!'* The new Secretary of State of War, Field Marshal Herbert Kitchener, was more realistic and forecast that this would be a long war, won only by victories on the continent. With only a small regular army and a national distaste for conscription, Kitchener knew that he needed volunteers in their hundreds of thousands to win a war like no other.

In its editorial of Friday 7th August, the local paper, the *Sevenoaks Chronicle* stated:

The terrible European War (so long regarded as one day inevitable by many deep think-
ers and students of foreign politics) is upon us and today the voice of local controversy
is stilled, and Sevenoaks has set out unhesitatingly and fearlessly to play her part in the
determination of England to strike a blow for righteousness, honour and justice.

It is estimated at a rough computation that from the immediate vicinity of this town
over 250 regulars, sailors, military and naval reservists, yeomanry and Territorials have
responded to Britain's call to arms and are all at this moment busily engaged in prepa-
ration for active service for King and Country.

Unlike previous conflicts, such as the South African wars of the late nineteenth century,
this would not be a war that was fought in some far off country with little impact on those
at home. Local people were affected by the outbreak of hostilities and actively involved in
supporting the national cause and preparing for events to come. The early arrival of the
wounded, foreign refugees, and the billeting of thousands of soldiers in the area meant that
from the start, the people of Sevenoaks would be well aware of the impact of the conflict as it
progressed. It would be hard not to notice the soldiers and the wounded in their midst and,
being well served by local papers, The *Sevenoaks Chronicle*, the *Kent Messenger* and the *Kent
& Sussex Courier*, residents were able to follow the progress of the national effort, their civic
leadership, and their neighbours who were now serving in His Majesty's forces.

Orders for General Mobilisation had been posted in Sevenoaks on the night of Tuesday
4th August at the Post Office and Police Station. Local Reservists, men who had been regular
soldiers and were held on the Reserve for a further five years, began to re-join the colours

**Troops marching through Sevenoaks, photographed by Walter Horncastle,
from the upper floor of his shop in the High Street.**

1.   The correct title of the regiment. For ease of reference it is referred to in the rest of the book in its shortened
     version.

from the following morning. The West Kent Yeomanry were ordered to assemble on parade and proceed to their headquarters some 12 miles away. The *Sevenoaks Chronicle*, reported that some 40 of the Yeomanry and their friends gathered in the centre of the town by the Fountain at the junction between London Road and the High Street and lustily sang 'Rule Britannia', followed by the National Anthem and three cheers for the King and three more for the Yeomanry itself. The *Kent Messenger* reported that large crowds had accompanied the departure of the Yeomanry, giving them an enthusiastic send off from the Royal Crown Hotel (which was located where the Stag Theatre now stands). Pupils from Lady Boswell's School marched down the High Street to witness their departure.

HIGH STREET. SEVENOAKS

The Fountain at the junction of London Road and the High Street

Seventy-three Territorials, men of four sections of G Company, the Sevenoaks contingent of 4th Battalion The Queen's Own Royal West Kent Regiment , also left the town on the Wednesday, accompanied by the town band, which had hurriedly left its engagement at the nearby Seal Flower Show to do so.

According to the *Chronicle*:

The company fell in at the Drill Hall (on Argyle Road, the home to B squadron of the West Kent Yeomanry and G Company of the 4th Battalion Royal West Kent Regiment) where the most enthusiastic scenes prevailed, and then headed by the Band, marched to Tub's Hill Station, between continuous lines of the inhabitants of Sevenoaks who had assembled in their hundreds to honour the departure of their 'Terriers'. The thunderous cheering of the multitude was continuous all the way along. Handkerchiefs were madly waved and not every eye was dry. There were humanely pathetic scenes too but enthusiasm was the key note.

Soldiers depart from Sevenoaks (Tubs Hill) railway station (*above & below*)

At the station, the Sevenoaks men joined their comrades from nearby Westerham and Orpington. The band performed the National Anthem from the platform. Large Union Jacks were waved from the roadway above.

The men were, noted the *Chronicle*, '*in excellent spirits and appeared in the pink of condition*'.

The paper reported that one local resident cleared the bookstall of papers and magazines and distributed them amongst the departing men. The 1/4th Battalion (formed of those Territorials who had volunteered for Foreign Service) left for India in late October 1914 with the remainder of the 44th (Home Counties) Division, where they replaced the units of the regular army stationed there, freeing them for service elsewhere.

Control of the Railway

Like all other railway companies, the South Eastern & Chatham Railway, had passed into Government control on 4th August. The priority now was the transport of troops and goods. Passenger traffic was not a priority and would be heavily curtailed during the war with priority given to soldiers, sailors, reservists, and recruits. Instructions were issued that no non-civilian was to be left behind by any train.

New recruits had already responded to the call to arms by enrolling in the Territorials but there was an awareness that perhaps a fear of losing their position permanently was making many young men hesitate before volunteering. One young apprentice at the *Sevenoaks Chronicle* wired his employers *'Have joined Territorials. Will my job be kept open?'* to which the paper assured its readers that it would.

Robert Mond, a local JP and owner of Combe Bank, Sundridge, whose stables were later to be given over as a VAD hospital, made it known that those in his employ who left to fight would find their position kept open for them and their time with the forces counted as continuous service. He urged other local employers to '*do their best in a similar direction*'.

The Rector of the parish church of St Nicholas, the Reverend John Rooker, noted that:

Our duty as Sevenoaks residents is to support Sevenoaks tradespeople.

How to provide relief for those who would be affected in different ways by the war was of concern to the Urban District Council. Some worried about the impact of local households cutting back on their usual expenditure and urged employers to keep on their staff. Consumers were encouraged to find work for their usual tradesmen and not to leave those who were unable to join up in financial difficulties. A War Relief Fund was established with the aim of raising donations that would be divided with 75% for local relief and the remainder sent to county funds. A meeting at the Drill Hall raised over £2000 alone.

Local shops such as the well-known firm of S.Young & Son, based at 110, High Street, took advertisements in the local press to assure its customers that, contrary to rumour, they were not reducing staff or closing down their factory but also appealed for customers to find any work possible for their employees. The store promoted its stock of goods approved by the Red Cross and West Kent War Clothing League, such as flannels, sheets and blankets, which were all available with a special 5% discount. At E.J. Payne, grocer and general stores on the High Street, parcels could be purchased and packed with essentials and other items for soldiers and sailors at the Front, ranging in price from 2s 6d, 5s and 10s. Letters and other items could also be included.

Many local residents turned to the church for support and worship. Special services were held at St Nicholas by the Rector. Large congregations heard him preach from Samuel (17, 47) 'The Battle is the Lords' at the morning service on Sunday 9th August, with a further service, for men only, in the afternoon attracting an estimated two to three hundred.

Open air services in the Market Place attracted a large attendance, with up to six hundred people coming together to listen to the Rector and other local religious leaders. While these services ended in mid-September, other events were held regularly in the Market Place on Saturday evenings, including talks on the meaning and cause of the war and '*What can be done by those who stay at home?*'

Lord and Lady Sackville, owners of Knole, the imposing house close to the heart of the town and a significant local employer, were keen to be seen to be doing their bit. Knole itself was offered as an annex to the two local hospitals. Lord Sackville served with the Yeomanry and donated the use of his car to the hospitals, while his wife was reported to have given hers up to the Red Cross. The *Chronicle* noted all this approvingly on 14th August:

> *Knole is, as usual, coming to the fore in a good cause and is setting an excellent example.*

Representatives of the town's civic leadership, such as J.F. Carnell of the District Council (whose brother George was, at 59, to become to town's oldest casualty when he was killed at Gallipoli in 1915), attended a county meeting at Maidstone, chaired by the Lord Lieutenant, the Marquess of Camden, which resolved to:

> *pledge itself to use its utmost endeavour to encourage recruiting of all those eligible men to serve in response to the appeal for 100,000 men made by Lord Kitchener, Secretary of State for War, and urges every district to take immediate steps to make the appeal known to young men in its area.*

Recruitment posters began to appear in the town, urging men to respond to Lord Kitchener's call and sign up for service in the battalions of the New Army. Advertisements in the local paper called for men aged between 19 and 30 to enlist for general service for three years or until the war was concluded, countering reported rumours that the terms were three years with the colours followed by a further nine with the Reserve.

Men were also needed as Special Constables and stretcher-bearers. Owners of motor-cars were urged to make them available to help transport men willing to enlist to the nearest recruiting depot at Tonbridge. Local recruiting offices were established in the High Street, St John's Parish Room and elsewhere to help those who wished to enlist or re-join and to arrange motor transport to Tonbridge as required. It was reported that the Tonbridge recruiting depot was anxious to secure recruits to meet demand for the six hundred Territorials now required for battalions of the Royal West Kent Regiment.

De Barri Crawshay of '*Rosefield*', Sevenoaks, inaugurated a system that would make use of the 130 cars that had been placed at the disposal of the authorities. The first big job was the transportation of men to the various recruiting centres. Crawshay was also jointly responsible for the telegraph and telephone lines in West Kent. A patrol of cars and up to 50 motorcycles, ensured that the wires were guarded against cutting or tapping.

Between 70 and 80 horses were bought and tethered in Knole Paddock, guarded by members of the National Reserve. Supper and breakfast was provided for the men, who were required to report for duty at the Police Station Yard with greatcoats, stout sticks, and blankets.

Spy Fever

Far from the German menace being solely a threat faced by soldiers abroad, accusations of enemy aliens were made rightly and wrongly, in the Sevenoaks District. German residents were required to register at the police station and many reports of German spies were made and investigated. Security was taken seriously. The Sevenoaks rail tunnel was guarded day and night with men on duty at each smoke shaft. Allegations, including one of suggested interference with the water supply at Dunton Green, were made to the police.

Although many of the accusations were groundless, the Sevenoaks Petty Sessions heard the case of John Stein of Kemsing who was charged with being an enemy alien and failing to provide the information required under the recent Alien Registration Order. Stein had been detained by a local gamekeeper and failed to produce his identification certificate when it was demanded. The court heard that the defendant had been living in Margate but that town was now a prohibited area with no German being allowed to live there without a police permit. As Stein was unknown in Maidstone he was refused a permit and travelled to London where, despite being told to call back for his certificate once sufficient enquiries were made, nothing further was heard of him until he was found in Kemsing. In court, Stein claimed that he had got lost and '*his head went wrong*' but was sentenced to six months in Maidstone Prison.

The Royal Crown Hotel.
Demolished in 1935, the Stag theatre now stands in its place

In Sevenoaks, Councillor Marshall, owner of the Royal Crown Hotel, received anonymous postcards which criticised his continued employment of a young Austrian, a decision which had been taken with the entire agreement of his staff.

Violet Rawnsley of One Tree Hill, Sevenoaks, felt compelled to write to the local paper after she was accused of working for the Germans and using her home as a safe haven for spies. Returning from a day in London she discovered five reporters from national papers waiting to question her on the rumours that she was German and that there was a 7ft high fence around the Rawnsley's home, which was being used as a wireless installation to signal to the enemy. With her husband on the staff of the Royal Engineers, having previously worked with the Red Cross in France, Mrs Rawnsley's repudiation of these scurrilous rumours was printed in full in the *Chronicle* in October 1914.

'Kitchener's Mob'

By early September it was estimated that around a hundred Sevenoaks men had enlisted in the ranks of the New Army. Known as 'Kitchener's Mob', these volunteers were recruited to all parts of the army. Contemporary news reports reveal the feeling that this was not sufficient. The tone of the *Sevenoaks Chronicle* became more strident on the issue, stating:

> *There are certainly large numbers of eligible bachelors still holding back from joining the colours, to the lasting discredit of our district.*
>
> *Young men of Sevenoaks, do you realise the force of this stigma? Are you going to permit the continuance? Do you know that if you are eligible physically, and able conveniently, to serve, and are nevertheless hanging back, you are helping this fair county as a whole to lose her old-time right and title to the first line of battle? Do you already know that Kent has already been pointed to as one of the counties where recruiting is slackest? It is up to you to remedy it.*

Such a tone was perhaps prompted by the paper's own report of a slur on the town carried in a 'certain London daily paper that no recruits were forthcoming after a recent recruiting meeting in the town'. Henry Forster, the MP for Sevenoaks, 'with characteristic energy and readiness, was prompt in his repudiation of this fallacy'.

This criticism no doubt stung and the new tone of the language for recruitment continued.

Appeals were also made for old soldiers and those too old for active service to enrol with the National Reserve. A cadet corps was established, while the local Rifle Club had also opened its doors to help residents learn to shoot with free instruction. Every man, noted

Leslie Mattholi in civilian life

The First Casualty

The first Sevenoaks casualty of the war was window-cleaner, and father of three, Leslie Mattholi.

He had joined the Norfolk Regiment in December 1901 aged 17 and served until 1911 when he became a Reservist. He had emigrated to Australia but returned and established himself in Sevenoaks. Leslie was recalled to active service with the Norfolk Regiment on 4th August 1914 and was killed three weeks later on 24th, aged 27. His body was discovered and buried in 1926.

the *Sevenoaks Chronicle* in one report '*can learn how to hit the bull's-eye and if he can hit the bull's-eye, he can hit the head of an arrogant Prussian*'.

Despite a generally good response to the call to arms by young recruits joining Lord Kitchener's army and of old soldiers to the local Reserve, it did not take long for further concern to be raised about attitudes amongst young unmarried workers and clerks. In its editorial on 28th August, the *Chronicle* echoed the Government's early slogan when it questioned whether the young and able-bodied, whose place at work could easily be filled by an older or weaker man, were not hiding behind a shield of '*business as usual*'. '*Deep down in his heart*', the paper judged, '*every young man in the country knows that the only place of honour for him is with the colours.*'

This line of argument was further developed by a patriotic appeal to women in an editorial that raised the prospect of conscription in the future, and repeated the question:

Women of Kent will you do your duty?
    If the men do not go willingly and the women do not help them to go, the Government will come and take them. This it has a right to do. Will you allow them to have such a humiliation?

Lilian Gilchrist Thompson, wife of the vicar of Kippington, Reverend Percy Thompson, also took this line at a large recruitment meeting held at the Drill Hall on Friday 28th August, presided over by local grandee and owner of Montreal Park, Earl Amherst. Mrs Thompson advised young women that there was only one suitable response if their young men were making excuses for not enlisting:

If you are not good enough to defend your country you are not good enough for me.

Those local political and spiritual leaders presiding at the meeting emphasised their own commitment to England's cause. The three sons of Mrs Thompson were already serving and Captain Herbert Knocker, the local recruiting officer, a married man at the upper age limit, was clear that he had put his own name down to be called when the time came for men of 40.

Mr d'Avigdor-Goldsmid reminded the crowd that the young men were wanted for the army. To laughter he said that it was no use saying '*I'll go when hopping is over. That is no laughing matter, for several young men have said that to me and that means that they are going to lose two or three valuable weeks*'.

Henry Forster, the Conservative Member of Parliament for Sevenoaks since 1892, was cheered when he mentioned that his eldest son was fighting at the Front whilst his son-in-law was serving with the Royal West Kent Regiment.

The *Chronicle* reported that this meeting '*was one of the best held in the County, and at the conclusion of which some forty young men put their names down, but altogether there have been some hundred gone down during the week*'. Of the forty men reported to have put their name's down to enlist after this meeting, fourteen unmarried men came from Earl Amherst's Montreal estate, two from Lord Hillingdon's service at Wildernesse, Seal, four from Chipstead Place and three from Lord Stanhope's estate at Chevening. The paper noted that those forty men made the journey to the Tonbridge recruiting office the Saturday after the meeting.

White Feathers

The giving of white feathers, primarily by women to young men they deemed to be shirking their duty, became a widespread practice across the country. Although there are no official reports of such activity in Sevenoaks, one local man, at the upper end of the age limit for recruitment, and performing a useful and respected role in the town, was presented with a white feather. This partly influenced his decision to join up, one that was regretted by many given his usefulness at home. A successful officer, he was later killed at the Front. The memory of his blood spattered uniform sent back to the family, caused lasting distress to those who saw it.

In subsequent weeks, there was an acknowledgement that some local would-be soldiers were being turned down because of the standards of the medical inspection required. The paper urged a more relaxed approach to the health of the male population.

While many men joined the Royal West Kent Regiment, it was reported in November 1914 that there had been an increase in applications for the Kent Cyclists' Battalion. The *Chronicle* noted *'a wave of patriotism having spread through the ranks of the numerous cyclist errand boys employed in the district, but many of the applicants have had to be refused, the lads being neither big enough, or in fact, old enough, to comply with the regulations'*. The paper carried details of how men could join a range of units, from the Royal Flying Corps at Farnborough, to the Household Cavalry, Royal Garrison Artillery, and the Army Service Corps. Local recruiting officer, Captain Knocker, would *'on behalf of all intending recruits, make all necessary written applications and assist men to join special corps on their personal application to him'*.

Early recruits from more prosperous families of Sevenoaks included the sons of the Rector, Kingsley Rooker, who later served with the Machine Gun Corps, and his brother, Guy, who joined the 4th Battalion Royal West Kent Regiment as a second lieutenant. Frank Robinson, son of Frank senior, a local councillor and owner of the Royal Oak Hotel, was serving with the Inns of Court Officer Training Corps and later appointed second lieutenant in 5th Battalion Northumberland Fusiliers. George Heslop, son of the Headmaster of Sevenoaks School, was also an early volunteer.

Sevenoaks men were also serving in the navy. Some were already experienced sailors having joined several years before. Local men were present at some of the most significant naval battles of the war, from Heligoland in 1914 to the Battle of Jutland in 1916.

The local press were soon full of news from those already seeing active service and from new recruits in the early days of their basic training. The first letter home from a Sevenoaks man who had seen action was from Thomas Porter of Redmans Place, Sevenoaks. Porter, who was serving in the Royal Navy, wrote at the end of August 1914 to tell his mother that he had seen action on-board HMS *Arethusa* at the Battle of Heligoland. His letters were published in the *Sevenoaks Chronicle* (see page 69).

Private J Turner, serving with 2nd Battalion Highland Light Infantry wrote from Melun (in the Seine-et-Marne department of France) on 2nd September 1914. His letter was the first account of a soldier having seen action to be published for general consumption in the *Chronicle:*

Just a few lines to let you know I am still going on well and in the very best of health. Since we arrived at Boulogne we have been marching nearly all the time, as much as 34 miles in a day. I have managed to keep in the ranks so far. We have been in action only once so far, but that was in Belgium. My Company were in trenches, and the German artillery fire was just too awful for words. You ought to have seen us when we did come out; every man was as black and dirty as if we had been sweeping chimneys. That was on August 24th, and now we are camping within 30 miles of Paris, having tramped the whole way. It is very hot out there, so we all look brown....

We have been retreating from Belgium and I believe the idea was to induce the Germans to come after us, because they had about four brigades of French troops here, and when we arrived yesterday we were able to have half a day's rest; then in the morning we were to attack, our Brigade (the 5th) in the centre, and two Brigades of the French on either flank, but here we are still, and the rumour is that the Germans have retreated. This is the best news of the war that I can tell you. I am sure that you know more than we do out here...

Shortly after writing this, Private Turner was wounded by gunfire and sent back to England to recuperate.

Undoubtedly the most significant of recruiting efforts came in late September, when Lord Kitchener's brother, Colonel Henry Chevallier Kitchener, spoke at a public meeting at the Market Place. Kitchener painted a vivid picture of the peril facing the country. Observing that Sevenoaks was now host to many wounded soldiers, he spoke of meeting one, who had told him that no sooner had they killed one German than two more took his place. Kitchener thundered:

Fellow countrymen! I have come here tonight to beg you, to implore you, to rally round the old flag.

Alluding to the possibility of German invasion and the occupation of the town by the enemy, Kitchener suggested that local men would feel compelled to resist

What then? Sevenoaks in flames. Women, old men and children at the mercy of a relentless foe. Therefore, oh! Men of Sevenoaks, I call on you to come forward to defend those you hold most dear. You cannot defend them at home. ...Our only hope is to aid France in her hour of need, and I call on you to do it. Now! Now!! Now!!!

After that stirring exhortation, another speaker, Colonel Simpson, asked the men in the audience to consider why they were standing in Market Place listening and not training and fighting for their country.

If further encouragement was necessary, the final speaker reminded the crowd that the son of their local Member of Parliament (John Forster, a second lieutenant in the King's Royal Rifles) had only recently been killed on 14th September, and that his spirit no doubt hovered over them at that present moment.

The emphasis on the need for eligible unmarried men continued; those who had signed

Frank Waydelin MC

up as Special Constables were urged to consider whether they should be enlisting with the regular forces instead. Letters to the local papers from men on active service continued to be used to encourage recruitment.

An appeal for men willing to join the Volunteer Training Corps appeared in the *Sevenoaks Chronicle* in August and September 1915

The Volunteer Training Corps (A Company, 5th West Kent Fencibles) launched a recruitment drive for men over military age to join their ranks. A meeting was held at the Lime Tree Hotel to attract new members. Men of every class signed up, including those who had previously been in the forces, such as their commandant, Frank Waydelin, who had been a captain in the Queen's (Royal West Surrey) Regiment. Early joiners included Archdeacon Dunkerley of the church of St John the Baptist. Primarily intended for home defence, recruits were assured that they would be unlikely to be called on for active service, except in a dire emergency, but some of their number went on to join the regular army. Waydelin himself enlisted with 9th Battalion Royal West Kent Regiment in April 1915 and served until he was taken prisoner in March 1918. He rose to the rank of captain and was awarded the Military Cross in 1918.

Letters home from serving soldiers often included a note of exasperation as to the number of volunteers that had come forward so far.

Second Lieutenant Robert Douglas Baird of 1st Battalion Rifle Brigade wrote from the Front in November 1914, to his parents at *'Holmleigh'*, Granville Road, Sevenoaks:

I'm with my platoon in my trench, and the Germans are in theirs 80 yards away, with only three little strands of barbed wire between us, and no chance of putting up more, and we believe they outnumber us 5 to 1….

Oh! how I wish some of those millions of men at home in England who say they cannot fight because of business, or other silly reasons, would realise how jolly near their little businesses etc. have been to being wiped out, how jolly near the whole blessed English Empire has been to being extinguished. And we are not yet out of the wood by a very long way, though the situation is better than it was a month ago. We must have men. Every day the necessity becomes more and more apparent and one almost wishes that half London could be blown up.

The papers talk of the 'calm spirit of the people.' Calm spirit be blowed! To be vulgar. What we want is men, and more men, and still more men, at once, before it is too late. I suppose we shall just pull through, or when it is too hopelessly late, then the papers will be able to talk of the grand rush of volunteers. People talk of the rottenness of the German Army. That's all rubbish. They are fighting with a fury and a dash that are quite unbelievable, and our work in checking them has called forth the highest praise from (General) French and the French. Do try to get men to join K's Army, even if you can only find one.

Baird had been educated at Winchester and commissioned in the Rifle Brigade from the Special Reserve on 14th August 1914. The same month he accompanied the battalion to France, commanding a platoon in 'A' Company. He was in the Retreat from Mons and the Battles of Le Cateau, Aisne and First Ypres. Baird was awarded the Military Cross for service in Egypt in the King's Birthday Honours in 1918.

By 1915 many Sevenoaks men had joined the colours. The local papers carried a weekly Roll of Honour and these were also displayed in churches and the public library. The churches, along with the papers, continued to urge eligible men to join up and many began to see that the introduction of conscription was perhaps inevitable. One officer wrote home from France a letter that was reproduced anonymously in the local paper to prick the consciences of those eligible young men who had not yet enlisted:

William Hicks

By November 1914, it was reckoned that 76 Old Boys of Lady Boswell's school were serving in the army or navy, many of whom had been members of the School's Rifle Club and were proving themselves to be fine marksmen. Many former scouts were also serving in the forces. William Goss Hicks, popular headmaster of Lady Boswell's school and a leading light of the new scouting movement in Sevenoaks, enlisted despite his age and standing in the community. Masters and boys presented him with a new wrist watch when he left the school. Hicks, who became as popular in the army as he was at home, died of his wounds in July 1917. His fiancé, Jessie Ellman, daughter of Alfred Ellman, an ironmonger on the High Street, was grief stricken. In 2017, an exhibition curated by his great niece, Jane Churchill, remembered William and Jesse. A hundred years after his death, a church service was held at St Nicholas church, where Hicks had once been a member of the choir.

LIEUT. W. G. HICKS.
260th Siege Batt. Royal Garrison Artillery.

The country is just beginning to look beautiful, all the Spring flowers out, and the hedges showing green; it makes me long for my dear home again; but it would not do for me to return with my task unfinished. I thank God I am fighting in France and not in England, and that the dear women of England are not drinking of the cup of bitterness and anguish that the poor people in this neighbourhood have drained to the very dregs.

The beautiful villages one mass of ruins and the household goods scattered, not one or two villages, but hundreds, on a frontage of 300 miles. Yes, 'Wake up England' and realise your peril before it is too late! Think it over, ye who are eligible!! Or would you prefer to see your grandfathers go out?'

Although Sevenoaks had suffered casualties, and some men had been killed accidentally or died of natural causes and buried locally, the death of Private Harry McCarthy was the first military funeral of a combatant to be held at Sevenoaks. Harry had been quick to enlist in Kitchener's New Army and served with the Duke of Cornwall's Light Infantry. Wounded in the spine at the battle of Neuve Chapelle in March 1915, he was buried in Greatness Cemetery with full military honours. A detailed report of the occasion was carried in the *Sevenoaks Chronicle*. Like many other local families, Mr and Mrs McCarthy had other sons serving and no doubt sympathy was felt for them throughout the town.

The people of Sevenoaks were further reminded of the sacrifices that had already been made when memorial plaques were unveiled at St Nicholas church to Lieutenant Horatio John Vicat of the Royal West Kent Regiment and Lieutenant William Guy Cronk of the The Buffs (East Kent Regiment), both young officers who had been killed in the early months of the war.

'Somewhere in France'

A letter from Private Raymond Hope Lawrence of Riverhead to his mother and sister was published in the *Chronicle* on 25th June 1915, striking in part a different tone from the usual.

The Company, he wrote from 'Somewhere in France' *'is stationed in a small town but this one is in the middle of a wood, and you can't imagine how the nightingales and various other beautiful songsters sing all day and night. It is very healthy and I simply love it. The trees are lovely and the daisies and water lilies wonderful. It is now nine o'clock on Wednesday night and within fifty yards of us there is a jay who is jabbering away. Three or four nightingales are singing to us all night long and the frogs keep up a continuous croak, croak which adds to the music. All this is close handy, but away in the distance the artillery are thundering their large shells and the quick firers and rifles can be heard cracking all night.*

Kentish Men

Like similar towns across the country, Sevenoaks had a tradition of military service. Men were recruited to the local militia, especially during times when there was a fear of invasion. The first company of Sevenoaks Volunteers was established at a meeting of the Royal Crown Hotel, presided over by Earl Amherst, in 1859.The company later became the 33rd

(Sevenoaks) Company of the Kent Rifles, and formed a guard of honour when the then Prince of Wales (later King Edward VII) visited Knole in 1866. All who joined were volunteers but were required to pay 10 shillings for the privilege. Training was held at Bethlehem Farm (formerly a farm in the High Street and now the site of the Oak Tree pub) and the militia could be seen on parade regularly. In 1897, the Drill Hill was opened in Argyle Road, as part of the celebrations of Queen Victoria's Diamond Jubilee. Within a couple of years, Sevenoaks men, like Silas George Copper, served in the South African wars as Queen Victoria's reign drew to a close.

The West Kent Yeomanry was also well known in Sevenoaks, holding its annual training in Knole Park in 1901, 1904 and 1908. When it did so for the last time before the war in 1912, 23 officers and 343 non-commissioned officers and men, were encamped in tents.

In 1907, the Government, under the leadership of Richard Haldane, Secretary of State for War, passed the Territorial and Reserve Forces Act 1907, which, from April 1908, merged the volunteer forces with the militia and the yeomanry. Local units, as in Sevenoaks, became part of the Territorial battalions of the local army regiment. Sevenoaks men became part of the Royal West Kent Regiment. Men who signed up to serve in the Territorials were not obliged to undertake overseas service but could choose to do so. By 1914, the Regiment had two Territorial battalions (4th & 5th).

A large number of Sevenoaks men served in the battalions of Royal West Kent Regiment during the war. At its outbreak in 1914, some were regular soldiers, like Horatio John Vicat, a lieutenant with 1st Battalion, then based in Dublin. Others were with the Territorials and away at their yearly camp, having to hurry back when the order for mobilisation came through. Then, as men were encouraged to join Lord Kitchener's New Army, many of these recruits naturally joined the Royal West Kent Regiment as the historic regiment of their own county. Others chose to join different regiments or were assigned to where need was greatest, and, later in the war, men could be transferred between regiments, to replace lost men. Some, like Jack Whyntie, began their service in the Royal West Kent Regiment but obtained a commission and became officers in a different regiment; the East Surrey Regiment in the case of Whyntie (see page 106).

Sevenoaks men who were on the Reserve (those who had previously served seven years with the Colours but who then spent a period of five years with the potential to be recalled if necessary) were mobilised in August 1914. George Homewood of 8, Bethel Road in the St John's area of the town, was recalled to 1st Battalion Royal West Kent Regiment on 5th August 1914 and was present at the Battle of Mons, where he was taken prisoner.

In October, the *Chronicle* reported that the numbers of the Royal West Kent Territorials (Reserve) billeted in the town had increased from 350 to 376, including men from Tunbridge Wells, Westerham and elsewhere. Regular new arrivals increased their number. According to the paper:

The daily programme is as follows: The Reveille is sounded at 5.30 and at 6.30 the company parade at the kitchen for hot soup and bread. Training operations for the day begins at 6.45 when physical drill is gone through on the Vine under the sergeant major. Breakfast of tea or coffee, bacon or fish with bread, butter, jam or cheese, is then served at 7.45. At 9.30 the battalion parades for drill or route march till one o'clock, then comes a very welcome dinner of roast or boiled beef with potatoes and another vegetable, with a second course where possible. The parade at 2.30 is the commanding officer's parade till tea at 5 o'clock, consisting of tea, bread, butter and jam.

The officers of the battalion have taken up their quarters at Southernwood, The Drive.

About a hundred of the men were kindly entertained to tea yesterday by Mr F Raper of The Hollies and other equally hospitable invitations have been extended. Sevenoaks is determined to see that her well behaved troops shall lack for nothing for their comfort. No less than seventy-five percent of the 4th Battalion have volunteered for active service and many of those parading daily in Sevenoaks, are only awaiting their nineteenth birthday and physical fitness to fly at the throat of the Germans.

On 25th September 1914, the *Chronicle* printed a letter, sent to the local recruiting officer, Captain H W Knocker, from a number of Sevenoaks recruits now training with the 6th Battalion Royal West Kent Regiment, one of the new battalions of Lord Kitchener's New Army, filled with local recruits. The battalion was put through its drill and training at Purfleet, Sandling, Hythe and Aldershot, before crossing to France in May 1915. The letter provided a detailed first-hand account of the experiences of many of the men, with an enthusiasm for their rations that suggested that some, at least, were being better fed than they had been in civilian life.

Dear Sir,

Just a line from the recruits you sent from Sevenoaks to this Regiment. We are all feeling well, fit and happy, and our officers do all in their power for our comfort. We have a large tent provided by the YMCA, where we can write our letters. They give us all writing materials free of charge; they have also provided a piano, and after duty we have some fine singing from the 'canaries' of the Battalion and we all let the chorus go with a bang.

Our Battalion is up to full strength and fully equipped, and besides uniform and equipment we have been issued with two sets of good underwear, cardigan jacket, sleeping cap, knife, fork, spoon and plate, razor and brush, hair, brush and comb, housewife, two towels, three pairs of socks, braces, and two pairs of good boots.

We sleep on average 16 in a tent, and when you get down you have got to stop there until Reveille, as there's hardly room to turnover. What a blessing it isn't mid-summer!

We are getting good food and plenty of it. Listen to this! Breakfast - bacon or corned beef, bread and tea; dinner - beef or mutton and potatoes; tea - bread, jam, cheese or butter. At supper time you have to 'square' the cook.

We turn out at five, clear tent, shake blankets and put kits tidy, and then have a wash and get on parade at six. We do about 8½ hours daily, including drilling, musketry, physical culture and lectures. We get together in the evening after duty and go down to the 7th Battalion to see if we can see any fresh faces from Sevenoaks, and here and there we see an old familiar face. Well, then it's 'How do you do?' and show them the cook house etc. If any visitors want to look round, well, we show them round (after they have stood us 'Woodbines' all round). If anyone comes down here ask for 'Woodbine Villa' and we will show them round. We are all qualified pilots (and smokers). Well, Sir,

I must close now, as it is nearly 'Lights Out' *(9.45) so with best wishes to you and the new recruits that are coming down from 'The Old Seven Oaks'*

Similar letters followed from other Sevenoaks men now in training or serving with other battalions of the regiment.

Private C Hayles of 1/4th Battalion Royal West Kent Regiment wrote home from Sandwich Bay, where he was billeted before departure to India:

I am getting on very well now. It was very strange at first, but I soon got used to it. We are doing a lot of work here, and we do not get much time to ourselves. We are quartered in the large house on the seashore. We are treated very well, with plenty of food, but very plain. We are making the most of that. My bed is the hardest I ever had, being the bare floor with one blanket, with a kit bag as pillow, but I am happy with it all. It is doing me a lot of good. I don't think it will be long before we go abroad.

Private A. Baker of 8th Battalion Royal West Kent Regiment wrote home from Maidstone:

I like this life very much. Of course, it was rather rough and ready for a time, but now we are very comfortable. We have plenty of drilling and gymnasium, and I seem to feel the benefit already. There are about 500 fellows in the Battalion, all real good fellows. We have every evening from 6 o'clock to go out, or for football, gymnasium or lectures. The life is very easy, practically all outdoor work, which will soon get one fit…

Most Sevenoaks men who were in the Territorials and volunteered for Foreign Service, served with 1/4th Royal West Kent Regiment in India throughout the war. Headmaster at Riverhead school, William Daniel Weth, had once served with the West Kent Yeomanry then transferred to the Kent Cyclists Battalion. Having enlisted with the Royal West Kent Regiment when war broke out, he wrote, as Quarter-Master Sergeant Weth, to the *Kent Messenger* in January 1916, from Jubbulpore, India.

Soldiering is all very well when one has been brought up to it, but requires some sticking when it comes suddenly, especially in a climate like India. I have been at it now since last September twelvemonth, and am beginning to like it.

One must live in India a long time before they can realise what a mighty Empire this is. It is a wonderful thing that so few white troops can hold it. The population of the native city here is over 100,000, and there are thousands in native villages on all sides. The white troops are strictly forbidden to enter the city or the villages. Personally I get on splendidly with the natives, and have made some friends among them. The lower caste Hindus or working classes seem timid, harmless sorts of individuals. It is with the educated Babus, etc., that any danger lies – men who are well educated and have travelled in Europe, and who can see and understand things for themselves.

We are in a great hunting district here. Tigers, panthers, jackals, hyenas, boars and monkeys are fairly plentiful. Jackals and hyenas come right into our barracks at night and make an awful row. Poisonous snakes are also common

I think all our battalion here would give anything to have a smack in to hasten the end, but we just stick it here till our rulers see fit to use us. Duty first, hard work, disease, malaria, poisonous insects, terrible heat and unknown dangers I don't mind but this confounded uncertainty is trying, and I should like to have a cut in somewhere for the Motherland where I was bred and born, and which holds all that is dear to me. I often think of our fishing expeditions, and the jolly times at Riverhead, and wonder will they come back.

Weth was stationed at Jubbulpore for two years before he was transferred to the Embarkation Department and spent nearly two years as Troopship Sergeant Major in Bombay.

Albert Kent had served with the 1st Battalion
Royal West Kent Regiment in Dublin before the war

Before the war, Private (later Acting Serjeant) Albert Kent, served with 1st Battalion of the regiment in Dublin, where he married a local woman in November 1913. Their son, also Albert, was born in August 1914. Albert senior served with the 2nd Battalion Royal West Kent Regiment in India. He wrote home to the Rector in early 1917, thanking him for a Christmas card:

I must tell you there are several Sevenoaks boys up here (in a station in India), and although we are not all close to each other, I am pleased to say they are in the best of health. When I visited the boys of Sevenoaks at (censored) they were having an enjoyable time there, and I had the pleasure of seeing them win the football cup. That was when I was on sick leave. I must say they well-earned it, as the Hants scored their goal in the first minute of the game but the Kent Regiment soon put up a quiet game and scored four goals before half-time. It was a match worth watching.

People back home in Sevenoaks were able to follow the fortunes of the Regiment through the local papers, letters home and photographs. In September 1916, the Essenhigh Corke photographic studio in Sevenoaks was displaying photographs of men of 1/4th Royal West Kent Regiment in the window of its London Road premises. Private Douglas Essenhigh Corke, serving with the Royal Signals in India, had been taking photos of the men with a small Kodak camera and many of his photos were displayed in his brother Henry's studio for public consumption, including a view of a temple, natives razor grinding, and a view of the bazar where men of the West Kents bought essential items and curios to send home. Henry and Douglas's brother, Lawrence, was also in India, serving with the Royal West Kent Regiment.

Nineteen year old Cyril Wood, a former pupil at Lady Boswell's School had enlisted on 1st September 1914. One of Lord Kitchener's recruits to the New Army, he served with 6th Battalion Royal West Kent Regiment. After training in England, Wood landed with the rest of his battalion in Boulogne on 1st June 1915.

Having marched through France, camping in barns and villages, he wrote to the *Sevenoaks Chronicle* from the frontline and highlighted how efficient the army postal service, crucial for morale, was:

I get the Sevenoaks Chronicle every week and this week received it in the trenches, so I am still in the knowledge of all that is happening at home.

Wood outlined some of his recent experiences:

We were in bivouac here a fortnight, awaiting orders as to which part of the firing line we should first be sent. On the Sunday we marched fifteen miles to a farm and here for the first time we could hear rifle fire distinctly, as before that we had only heard guns and you can guess it caused just a little bit of excitement. The following night we went up into the firing line attached to another regiment for instruction but since then we have held our own trenches.

Our first experience of this was being welcomed in by shrapnel, and directly after this the Germans blew up a mine in front of us which, had it been under our trench as they supposed it to have been, would have sent us well on the way to glory; as it was, we escaped with a good shaking. This was followed by a good supply of rifle grenades and trench mortars, which unluckily injured some of our men, and we were destined to lose some more before leaving the trenches, which, after we did, were lucky enough to get sent back to the nearest town for a six day rest, and, I might add, this is the only one of its nature since coming out here.

In some places the German trenches and ours are very close, and on one occasion we were only thirty yards away, at other times, three or four hundred yards. it was quite easy to throw bombs from one trench to the other, and this was done to some effect. Also, one could hear, laughing, talking and singing quite distinctly, and not a few times

'Tipperary' was being practised, for the trenches were being held by the Saxons, who by far are the most peaceful, not firing unless fired upon. But the Prussians and Bavarians, especially the former, stop at nothing.

As the battalions of the New Army were created it was thought that men would be more naturally inclined to serve if they could do so with their friends and colleagues. Thus the so-called Pals Battalions were formed. Usually associated with the north of the country, there was, however, a City of London Stockbrokers Battalion, part of the Royal Fusiliers. The concept was not replicated in Kent, but many men, in Sevenoaks and throughout the county, enlisted together and served with their friends, neighbours and colleagues in the new battalions of the Royal West Kent Regiment, particularly the 6th and 7th. Thus Sevenoaks men, like Cyril Wood, found themselves in training and serving abroad with former school friends and fellow members of the scouts or Church Lads' Brigade, church choirs, and bell-ringers.

Local men serving in these battalions were present at some of the most significant actions of the regiment during the war. Sixteen men of 1st Battalion were killed and are remembered on the Sevenoaks War Memorial, including Lieutenant Henry Arthur Poland and Private Thomas Francis who were both killed at the taking of Hill 60 in April 1915. Fred Gilks was killed on 13th July 1916, the same day as Lawrence Bowles and James Pettitt. All were serving with 7th Battalion when they were killed at the Capture of Trones Wood, an action which was part of the battle of the Somme.

Fred Gilks, who was killed on 13th July 1916

The Vine War Memorial lists 16 Sevenoaks men who had enlisted with 6th Battalion of the Royal West Kent Regiment, including brothers, Allan and Harry Stevens of Cobden Road. A further 13 townsmen were killed while serving with the 7th Battalion of the Regiment.

In all, 68 Sevenoaks men who served in one of the battalions of the Royal West Kent Regiment were killed or died of their wounds. Of these fallen men, the bodies of 29 were never found.

Letters from the Trenches

By mid-1915, the tone of the letters home that were published had begun to change. The eagerness of new recruits gave way to outlining the grim realities of the conflict. Gunner George Burgess of the Royal Field Artillery wrote home in September 1915 of his experience of being gassed. Poison gas was a new weapon, first used by the Germans during the Second Battle of Ypres in April 1915. Burgess wrote:

I am getting plenty of practice now leading the Germans a dance; they think they are at the top of the tree, but we are too many for them. They have tried every evil device they thought of and failed. The last one was awful. One could hardly stand against liquid fire. Then gas is bad enough. I have tasted that stuff and it's not very nice. It is rather a sensation when the word goes round, 'Look out, boys, the gas is coming'. On go our helmets, and one cannot help smiling. We look like a 'Black Hand' gang. Never mind, the day of reckoning is coming for them; it only makes our chaps go for them all the more when they come to gripe.

Lieutenant A E French, 6th Battalion City of London Regiment, wrote home in April 1915:

Trench life is very exhilarating in a way. One's nerves are constantly at the highest pitch, but all through this the men are happy as can be. They cook their food in these trenches – fire, support, and reserve trenches. In many cases the trenches we have occupied have only been about 50 and 80 yards from the Germans. The thought of it keeps one awake, but in reality the sleepless nights and constant look-out is very lowering, and I can tell you the men are only too pleased to get their sleep when they have been relieved by another battalion.

Private George Scothern of the Rifle Brigade wrote home to his father, Sanitary Inspector for Sevenoaks, in May 1915.

I have just been relieved from the trenches. Where I had my first taste of fire, and a rare game it is. We have had some of the hardest fighting of the war. The Germans attacked us but we beat them off, not without losing a few pals, however. The German shell fire was terrific, but it was surprising how one gets to disregard it when firing at the enemy. …The country here is glorious but it is a shame the way it is blown to pieces by shellfire.

We are at present resting at a lovely little Belgian farm, one of the very few still standing, and we have a big barn full of nice clean straw. Last night was the first night that we had been able to sleep for sixteen days, as we have been in the trenches all that time, and while there we have to work during the night and try to sleep in the day-time. A lot of the time we were in the first line trenches and my word! We had it warm. I was rather lucky for when we were attacked at close quarters I got my bayonet shot to pieces as I was going to fire, and a small piece of shrapnel hit me in the shoulder, but did not penetrate beneath the skin. You would have laughed to see the Germans run each time we started on them, but some have got pluck, for they came up three times. They walked across the fields in extended order as if on parade, with the German guns full on them, sending hundreds of shells.

In a later letter, having asked for goggles with which to protect his eyes from poisonous gases, he wrote:

It looks to me as if the war will soon be carried on by the chemists and not soldiers, judging by their uses of gases and different concoctions in the shells.

And again

Our artillery replied but it is not very effective. It is about time to say 'Wake up, England.' People grumble about our infantry losses, but one cannot expect much else if they are not backed up properly by big guns because workmen go on strike for more money.

Most of the letters, published in local papers, detailed experience of the Western Front but occasionally men wrote from other parts of the world. Private Charles Perrie of 25th Service Battery, Legion of Frontiersmen was serving with the British East Africa Expeditionary Force and wrote home to his brother, who lived on Camden Road, in October 1915. Men in the non-European theatres of war faced different challenges:

We have now relieved fellows in about the worst fever district out in this country. It is extremely hot, and the whole countryside is one mass of dense bush, very difficult to cross, more so because every bush or plant almost is one mass of prickles, rivalling a gooseberry tree in quantity, and easily beating it in quality. It is a country in which expert bushmen are required, and of course the German Askans are as such. One has to keep his eyes well open in case of ambush and such things.

On a long patrol we get bully beef. We read of rum rations and minor sundries in France, but we don't need anything like that; anyway, they don't appear....

I am afraid that the numerous charitable institutions who send things to the Dardanelles and France, have forgotten us here out in 'No Man's Land'. We feel this especially as those fellows are occasionally able to get home on furlough, whilst we are not. We seldom see white people, especially girls (haven't seen one for weeks), and, personally, haven't been in a town since leaving England.

A different tone was struck in June 1916 when Ezra Bourne of Kippington Lodge, Sevenoaks, received through the post, a tortoise, sent by his son, Lance Corporal Frank H Bourne, from Gallipoli. Bourne, who had emigrated to Australia and was serving with the Australian Force, took the tortoise with him from the Dardanelles when he travelled to Egypt. From there the animal was posted to his old home in Sevenoaks. According to the *Kent Messenger*, which printed a brief report on the story '*it arrived none the worse for its long journey. The little animal was sent in a small tin box, and apparently subsisted on the paper in which it was wrapped*'.

Prisoners of War

Some local men were taken prisoner by the enemy. In July 1915, the *Chronicle* interviewed William 'Shelley' Constable of the Royal Army Medical Corps. Back at home in Moor Road, the paper questioned him about his experiences:

I was taken on August 26th after the Battle of Mons, when we were collecting the wounded, and altogether about 270 officers and men of the medical services were captured. We were taken by rail to Sennelager (a prisoner of war camp) and during that journey we suffered much hardship. We had a shocking time both at the hands of the German people and also from the soldiers of our escort.

Whenever we got to a station and a train was passing we were laughed and jeered at and bustled about. For thirty-six hours we got nothing to eat or drink, no food of any kind. Then they gave us some hard and dark stale bread to eat and water to drink. We were called 'English swines' and other names which we could not understand.

Constable recounted how he slept with around 100 to 150 other men in leaky tents:

The weather was dry at first, but when winter came it was awful. The snow and ice penetrated the tents, which were full of vermin and the blankets they gave us were disgustingly dirty. This lasted right up until Christmas. Then they put us into huts which had been specially built for us. The sanitary arrangements were awful. We slept, ate, washed, and lived in the same hut. There were no recreation rooms, no games or anything like that provided.

After commenting about the poor food, Constable set out how he and his fellow prisoners were made to work:

We got up at six o'clock in the morning at first but for the last four months it was four o'clock. We drank our coffee and were then marched off in gangs to work about four miles away, eating our bread as we marched. We had to make roads, and haul timber, work which tried some of us very much owing to our poor food. Our boots wore out and we were given clogs, which crippled my feet and many of my comrade's. We came into dinner at one o'clock then went out again till four or five. We had the rest of the day to ourselves.

Constable was released on 27th June 1915, and sent via train to Brussels, where he and others were handed over to the care of the Red Cross.

The *Sevenoaks Chronicle* saw his '*plain and unvarnished statement*' as '*yet another example of Teutonic cynicism and disregard for the chivalry and courtesies of war*'.

Toward Conscription

By the autumn of 1915 the Government, though shying away from the introduction of conscription, knew that the flow of volunteers was diminishing. It had raised the upper age limit for recruitment from 38 to 40 in May that year, followed by the passing of the National Registration Act in the July. The Act established a register of men aged 15 to 65 designed to reveal how many men not already serving in the forces there were, along with their trade or employment. The register revealed that there were 5 million such men, with about 1.6 million in protected trades.

The War Office subsequently stated that voluntary enlistment would end in December 1915 and that men could either enlist voluntarily before then or choose to attest and be

Young Patriots

While patriotism and duty was urged upon men of military age, the *Chronicle* noted that the younger generation were demonstrating this virtue. In December 1915, Harry Lampkin and John West, pupils at St John's School, spoke on behalf of their fellow pupils when they requested that the money usually spent on prizes be donated to the local VAD hospitals.

called up when needed. Men who attested were identified according to their marital status and sorted into groups based on their age. The Group Scheme became better known as the Derby Scheme after Lord Derby who, as Director General of Recruiting from October 1915, was responsible for it. These men were held on the Reserve and given a grey armband, with a red crown in the centre, to symbolise their readiness to serve. They continued in their civilian life until they were called up. The Scheme was a halfway house to conscription.

In its editorial of 29th October, the *Sevenoaks Chronicle* stated:

Although it would perhaps be exaggeration to state that the whole Allies fate in the War depends on the results of the great British recruiting canvas, which started this week, it is none to affirm that Great Britain herself depends upon them for her future international status.

The paper reported that canvassers were urgently required for the Derby Scheme in the Sevenoaks District and should contact Mr Potter, Hon Secretary of the local Parliamentary Recruiting Committee, at his London Road address.

By mid-November the *Chronicle* was commenting on the success of the Scheme, noting that:

It's an undoubted fact that a number of men are joining the Reserve who have hitherto held themselves exempt from all service obligation whatever by reason of home or business ties.

The *Kent Messenger* also noted that the success of the Scheme in Sevenoaks was '*highly satisfactory. Evidently the men who had not been attested were determined to present themselves at once, and not undergo the stigma of the possibility of being a conscript*'.

A Recruiting Office for Sevenoaks and District was established under a Captain Elliot. Local recruits could be medically examined and attest for any branch of the army, without having to make the journey to Tonbridge.

The eventual failure of the scheme to produce the numbers required paved the way for the introduction of conscription in 1916.

The Military Service Act which introduced conscription was passed by Parliament in January 1916 and came into force that March. Only a few months later, the architect of the new volunteer army, Lord Kitchener, was dead, drowned when HMS Hampshire was sunk that June. The flags of the parish church and other public and private buildings in Sevenoaks were flown at half-mast as a mark of respect to Lord Kitchener when news of his death reached the town.

The Oldest Soldier

The oldest soldier from Sevenoaks who saw active service and is remembered on the War Memorial is 59 year old Francis George Carnell, who was killed at Lone Pine, Gallipoli in 1915. But Francis was not the oldest Sevenoaks man to wear uniform during the war.

Frederick Tokeley had run the Royal Oak Tap public house in Sevenoaks for a number of years. Tokeley was born in Essex in 1850. The 1901 census shows him as landlord of the Royal Oak Tap, living with his wife, Eliza, and three of his five children – Eleanor, Charles and Florence. Eliza died in 1908 and was buried in the churchyard at St Nicholas. Tokeley claimed to be 56 and working as a coachman when he enlisted with the Royal Army Veterinary Corp in May 1915, aged 65. He served with the RAVC from May 1915 until February 1918, when he was discharged for being no longer fit for active service, having spent over two and a half years in France. He was occasionally mentioned in the *Sevenoaks Chronicle* when home on leave. The paper reported his correct age and that he would stay with his daughter, Mrs Judd, who ran the Railway Hotel, Bat & Ball. He died in July 1919 from chronic bronchitis (aggravated by exposure on active service), aged 68.

Francis George Carnell (1859-1915)

Frederick Tokeley (1850-1919)

With so many members of the town band having volunteered, it was eventually suspended in June 1916. A Roll of Honour naming those members serving was framed and hung in the band room. Many former members wrote back home to the band's Hon. Secretary, Albert Killick. Alfred Holland, based somewhere in England with the Ordnance Department wrote:

Although so far away, my heart is still in it, at least the musical part of it. And I cannot tell you how much I miss it. Still, I hope I shall be back with you before this season is out. The clouds are clearing fast…How many members have joined up now? And how are they all getting on. I could have a few minutes on the clarinet occasionally, but I am not forgetting anything and an occasional blow on a flute keeps me in practice very nicely.

Another former member, Gunner T Cripps wrote from somewhere abroad and outlined his exploits having travelled all through Christmas until they reached their destination at the end of January:

> *We are not able to go out many miles on account of not having any water supply…the water we have to drink is sea water, which runs through a large water condenser, the pipes running out to the sea. I can't say our rations are very grand, living mostly on bully beef, biscuits, cheese and jam. Sometimes we get bread but not very often.*

Referring to the number of single men still in England, he commented, *I think it is a disgrace having to make conscription before they can get them.*

Soldiers in Town

From the early days of the war, increasing numbers of soldiers began to be billeted in Sevenoaks, staying either in tents in Knole Park, the Wildernesse Estate and Bligh's Meadow, or being assigned rooms in private houses. Among the first troops to be billeted in Sevenoaks were many new recruits, from the 1/4th Battalion of the Royal West Kent (Reserve) in September 1914, including men from D and E companies from Tunbridge Wells. In October the Council was asked to make plans to accommodate 13,000 men of other regiments, and 2000 horses, space for 6000 of the men being found in the surrounding villages. In its Friday 30th October edition, the *Kent and Sussex Courier* reported that:

> *Every empty house and all available public and other buildings have all been taken for the accommodation of the troops, while practically every house has one or more soldiers in them.*

The available evidence suggests that the majority of Sevenoaks residents took in soldiers without complaint. A few men could be billeted together in the smaller houses, while a

---

Salute to a Crimean Veteran

Joseph Baker of '*Lynmouth*', The Drive, Sevenoaks, was a well-known local veteran of the Crimean War. Baker flew the Union Jack and the flags of his allies from his home on significant days, from Royal Birthdays to naval and military victories during the war. When he died aged 89 in 1922, his obituary in the *Chronicle* recorded that:

> *One of the most memorable moments of his life was when a large body of troops passing along The Drive on their way to the camp at Wildernesse were halted by their Commanding Officer, who recognised in the familiar figure standing at the gate one of his own uncle's comrades-in-arms in the Crimea and at his bidding thunderous cheers were given for the brave old warrior.*

Baker was buried with full military honours at Greatness Cemetery.

larger number could be housed in the grander residences of Sevenoaks. Billeting was not enforced by the authorities on any home where it would cause, according to the *Chronicle*, '…*the least suspicion of serious domestic inconvenience or difficulty*'.

Those who did offer space to billeted men were entitled to receive 9d per night for lodging if a bed was provided, with extra payments for providing breakfast, dinner or supper. The rate for officers was 3s per night, although they were required to pay for their own food. Arrangements were made to make the new public bathing facilities on Eardley Road open to the men billeted in the town, as well as local residents; according to the *Chronicle* in January 1915 '*the local troops were soon splashing about*'.

Mrs Johnson and her daughter pose with men of the Middlesex Regiment

Mr and Mrs Johnson of '*Langley*' on Mount Harry Road, with its several bedrooms, offered billets for soldiers from the Loyal North Lancashire Territorials and the Middlesex Regiment and posed happily for photos with several of the men.

Edmund Gillow, a Liverpool teenager of 17 had enlisted has soon as he could and, as a private in the 5th Battalion Liverpool Regiment, spent a few weeks in Sevenoaks, which he recalled in his unpublished memoirs, written in 1925:

> *Here good news awaited us; we were to be billeted in occupied houses, a distinct improvement on tents and waiting rooms. Two other chaps and myself were allocated to the house of a cab driver. A real old Dickens character this chap, and he and his wife made things very comfortable for us while we were under his roof.*
>
> *Strict training for active service was now begun, and discipline was tightened up all round. Non-commissioned officers with whom we had been accustomed to share our jokes and pleasantries, now glared and threatened if we did not address them by their proper handles. Lance Corporal, Sergeant or whatever it was. It didn't matter how long you had been calling him 'Bill'; you had to forget it now. Of course one came across a few N.C.Os who didn't think they were Field Marshals but they were the exception.*

Private Edmund Gillow
5th Battalion Liverpool Regiment

We performed drill route marches and field manoeuvres enough to satisfy a glutton, and our night operations in the famous Knole Park, had the deer scared stiff.

It is a tough bit of country round about Sevenoaks, the hills being guaranteed to reduce anybody to a grease spot who had to carry a pack up them. The town itself was about as lively as a ladies' sewing class, so that we were not sorry after a few weeks to be moved off to Canterbury.

The Vine Pavilion was opened in mid-September 1914 as a temporary branch of the YMCA for the use of the increasing number of soldiers billeted in the town. Ping pong tables had been provided with games and refreshments and an appeal was made for the temporary loan of other items, such as a piano, hearthrugs, tables and other things that would make the space more comfortable for the men. A YMCA Recreation Room was also established on Bethel Road.

In an editorial on 23rd October 1914, the *Sevenoaks Chronicle* stated that:

Very naturally private billeting is not to the taste of everybody (the military themselves are anything but enamoured with it) but these are times in which we must all look for some little inconvenience or discomfort, and it is all very much to be preferred, surely, to something infinitely worse. Military necessity and exigency come before everything just at present (and very rightly so), but both civil and military authorities have been most kind and considerate throughout. …Anyhow, gallant British Tommies are three thousand times more welcome in any numbers than half-a-dozen Prussian pigs.

The billeted soldiers were generally very well received. The Sevenoaks Chamber of Trade expressed *'very strong approbation of their behaviour'* in November 1914. Reported in the

1/5th Battalion (Territorial), King's Own Royal Lancaster Regiment digging trenches and on parade in Knole Park

Chronicle, committee member, George White, *'spoke very highly of the good gentlemanly behaviour of the Liverpools and also of the West Kent Regiment during their presence in the town, and of the benefit it had been to the trade of the town to have them billeted here. Speaking of the 5th, 6th, and 8th Liverpools, he said these troops did credit to the town to which they belonged and the Hon. Secretary was desired to write to the Commanding Officer of each of these battalions, expressing the appreciation of the Chamber of their conduct whilst they were in Sevenoaks'.*

The author, Rudyard Kipling, spoke to some of the troops billeted in the town when he visited Knole Park in the autumn of 1914. A report of this was printed in some newspapers although not in the *Sevenoaks Chronicle*. Cycle-Sergeant F. C. Callis, from Bolton and serving with 5th Loyal North Lancashire Territorials, in training at Sevenoaks wrote:

Our battalion turned out in full marching order and proceeded to our usual practice ground, Knole Park. The cycle section marched in the rear of the column, and an ordinary-looking man came to me and asked me a lot of particulars about the battalion.

He told me he had seen a lot of soldiering in his time, and said he must confess that our men struck him as being about the smartest on the march he had ever seen outside Regulars.

**Don't be Alarmed,
the 5th King's Own Lancs
are on guard at Sevenoaks.**

He asked me for so many particulars about them, and also about their billets, that I thought I should detain him as a sort of spy. I excused myself and rode off to the head of the column and informed one of our majors as to the nature of the conversation, etc., and took the man later to the major, and then left them and took my section on road-finding.

An officer of ours stopped me today and laughingly asked me if I knew whom I had tried to put under arrest. I answered in the negative, and he told me it was Rudyard Kipling.

Local licensed premises were required by magistrates to close at nine o'clock, pleasing temperance campaigners such as Lilian Gilchrist Thompson, but angering others who saw this as an unnecessarily prohibitive, especially as some noted that the restrictions in neighbouring towns were not as severe. The Urban District Council, responding to public sentiment, questioned the wisdom of the decision by the local magistrates but it was upheld and remained in place.

Following on quickly from the heated debate about public house closing times came a controversy started by the Federation of the Church of England Men's Society which suggested that, except on Saturday's, given the large military presence in the town, a curfew bell should be rung by the churches at eight-thirty, after which no woman should be out of doors. The suggestion was given short shrift by the majority of Sevenoaks residents. Several wrote to the *Chronicle*, signing their letters as 'an outraged father' or 'Tradesman's wife and mother'. A 'Shop Assistant ' wrote to the paper in forthright terms:

Curfew bell, indeed! It is an insult to both our Army and every woman in Sevenoaks! What is a shop assistant to do, working until eight o'clock, for the fresh air which is so necessary after her day's work?

The proposal was not adopted.

The New Year of 1915 saw more efforts to provide comfort and entertainment for the troops. A YMCA hut was opened between Hitchen Hatch Lane and Mount Harry Road. A 100 feet long by 30 wide, the new wooden building could provide a respite for many of the young soldiers who were stationed in the town. A temporary YMCA hut in front of the Vine Pavilion, which opened later in the year, was also popular with troops in the town. Concerts, lectures, entertainments and sustenance were all provided.

The author, Henry Williamson, later to be famed for his novel, *Tarka the Otter*, attended an officer training course in Sevenoaks in May 1915 and was billeted in the Royal Crown Hotel. Williamson wrote of his experiences in his novel, *A Fox Under My Cloak*, part of his fifteen volume 'A Chronicle of Ancient Sunlight'. Recalling how young officers drilled their own squads in front of Knole, the novel's hero, Philip Maddison, remembered how one King's Sergeant of Foot Guards put his men through their paces. Williamson wrote that '*terrible sounds of command tore out from his throat, echoing back from the grey stonework of Lord Sackville's historic mansion*'.

On the whole, both town and visitors coped well with these arrangements. While there were grumblings about how some soldiers were addressing local women or whether there should be a curfew, the people of Sevenoaks welcomed these strangers in their midst. They did their utmost to make them feel welcome with gifts and fundraising.

In January 1915, the *Sevenoaks Chronicle* printed an article by the paper's own editor (Sydney) Thornton Shaw, on *How Our Troops Fared at Christmas*. The article was, in fact, more of a guide to the men of the north and what was perceived as their strange habits:

You have got to know the average Northerner before you can hope to understand him. He is, by nature, hardy and brusque, he often omits to lift his cap (which he wears in great preference to a bowler hat) to his lady friends and when he is not on military duty he has an inherent objection in saying 'sir' to anybody on earth. But he possesses a heart as big as the wide world itself...

He continued:

And if some of them seem just a little bit uncouth you must forgive them. And they have done Sevenoaks heaps of good in the matter of trade. Ask any tradesman you like...

Shaw noted that the residents of Sevenoaks had raised £710 to ensure that the soldiers present in the town during Christmas enjoyed the festivities, with lavish amounts of food and entertainment; one contingent of 25 men '*polished off an entire pig between them...as my informant (an officer) laughingly remarked 'only a collier could have done it'.*

All of the men, wrote Shaw, were grateful but also wistful for the lives they had left at home, one corporal remarking, as he posted home a box of chocolates to his wife:

'Ah'd reyther 'uv bin up at whoam, if ah'd had nowt but kippers'.

Shaw himself, who had long been a member of the Territorials, was called up in April 1916 aged 39.

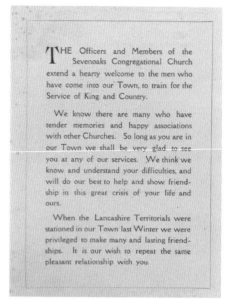

Local churches welcomed soldiers billeted in the town and invited them to services

Among the men of the King's Own Royal Lancaster Regiment billeted in Sevenoaks was young Private John Wilkinson. Not yet 18, he had joined the Territorials in 1912. He was mobilised in August 1914 and went to the south of England with the rest of the battalion. John wrote home regularly from Sevenoaks from his lodgings at 6, Serpentine Road

December 1914.

Dear Mother and Father,

Just a line to hope you are in the best of health as it leaves me at present. I received your letter and the money. I thank you for the money it will come in very useful. I have not received the parcel yet, perhaps it is on the road but I think I was very lucky to get the letter. Well mother we are going in very strict training down here we have a parade at seven in the morning till eight, then from nine till one, then from two till half past four it is all field training on the double so father will understand what we are doing.

They are making us all grow moustaches you should see mine now it would do you a bit of good. If we shave it off we get about fourteen days at Chelsea and I don't want that. I have seen big chaps go there and come back like old men. I think they are sending all the home service men to Blackpool I don't think there is a man in the regiment who isn't sorry he signed on for Foreign Service, especially the sergeants. We are getting messed about that much but I not worrying you get out of that. We will be alright as soon as we get out we won't have half as much to do. I think we are going out about January the fourth.

It is hard lines on the woman we are billeted on they have made her clear three rooms for sixteen of us and she has to look after her father he is nearly dying and she has to cook our meals for us and there is bound to be a bit of noise when we all get in but she can't get out of it because she is a nurse under the government. She was at the front in the South African War and she doesn't half tell us some tales.

She said her husband was fighting at the same time and they fetched a dead man in one day and she was told off to lay him out and when she pulled the sheet from his face it turned out to be her husband. I think it is hard lines having to put up with us now.

Well mother I haven't much more to say so I will close with best love to all, Flo, Dot, Baby, Aunt Lilly, Father and yourself mother, from your loving son Jack.

xxxxxxxxxxxxxxxxx

John Wilkinson did not live to face the enemy. He died on 12th January 1915 at the age of 17 of meningitis, shortly after leaving Sevenoaks. His body was returned to Barrow-in-Furness. An officer wrote to his mother that he gave his life for his country as *'bravely as any who die in the fighting line'.*

In January 1916, the question of whether military football should be played on Sundays on the new recreation ground at Hollybush Lane was discussed by the Council. After discussion of bylaws, propriety, the quiet enjoyment of near neighbours entitled to their rest, and the needs of the military, the Council voted to allow football to be played on Sunday afternoons,

Football matches were regularly played between different regiments
at the Hollybush recreation ground

with the proviso that there was to be no shouting. Naturally the decision provoked much discussion and correspondence in the newspapers. If soldiers could play, why not others; would a band playing music be more appropriate? The Rector objected to the decision but the Council considered that as the recreation ground lay outside of his parish and the relevant incumbent had no objection, then there was no need for permission to be withdrawn. An anonymous lance corporal pointedly asked a question of the Rector via the pages of the *Kent Messenger*. '*Does it not occur to the Rev Rooker*' he wrote '*that we have to break our Sabbath many times in the course of our duties, especially at the Front?*'.

Local residents remembered the men who had been billeted with them long after they had left. In 1918, the *Sevenoaks Chronicle* was still carrying reports of men who had lived amongst them. In February 1918 there was news of Lieutenant Harold Parker, formerly a sergeant major in the King's Own Royal Lancaster Regiment who had been billeted in the town in 1915; he had been wounded but was recovering well. Lieutenant George Wilkinson, had been in the Loyal North Lancashire Regiment when he was billeted in Victoria Road, Sevenoaks, he had since been commissioned in the Tank Corps. In that March there was news of Lance Corporal Wells of the Middlesex Regiment, who had lodged with Mrs Quinnell on Cobden Road. He and many other 'former friends' were wished a speedy recovery in the paper when news of their wounds was received.

$\sim$

Part Two

REFUGEES & WOUNDED

Belgian Refugees

In 1914 the *Sevenoaks Chronicle* reported in its Friday 16th October edition that:

> *Since the fall on Antwerp, the Belgian refugee has really begun to make himself felt as part and parcel of London's population; we may fairly add, of Sevenoaks population too.*

The paper noted that Belgian refugees had begun to arrive a few days before. It was estimated that there were already 1200 in Kent overall, with 41 being sent to the Cornwall Hall VAD hospital, 27 to St John's Hall, 30 to Chevening, and 16 to the Wildernesse VAD at Seal.

According to the article:

> *Most of the wounded are in the convalescent stage, but some have shrapnel and bullet wounds, more especially shrapnel. In some cases these brave fellows had not had their clothes off for three days, and some had not had their wounds dressed for three to six days.*

Belgians.

Over the next few weeks and months, the paper highlighted how local people were engaged in raising money and collecting clothes for the refugees already in their midst. On 23rd October, the *Chronicle* reported a whist drive being held in the Weald for the destitute Belgians Fund, while Mr Frank Robinson let it be known that the Electric Cinema on the High Street was admitting Belgian refugees and soldiers in to the mid-week and Saturday matinee for free, to see such films as '*A Sporting Chance*' and the patriotic '*Your County Needs You*'.

The same edition of the paper carried names of some of the first refugees, as well as those Sevenoaks residents who had opened up their homes to receive them. Madame de Chauvaux-Marlier, together with her four children and two other adults were staying at Bulimba, the grand residence of the Hemmant family; Madame Chainage-Rooms, of Liege, was staying at *Ashgrove* with her children, and Mrs Hawkes, an English refugee from Insterburg, was staying at 10, Eardley Road, her husband being interned at Spandau fortress.

J S Richardson, Secretary of the Working Committee of the Sevenoaks War Relief Fund (who was later to be killed on active service and is remembered on the town War Memorial) wrote to the paper asking for those hosting or otherwise responsible for any refugees in the town, to register them by completing a form to aid in the compilation of a national register.

A letter also appeared in the paper from Mr Swanzy, Chairman of the Urban District Council. He appealed for more means to deal with the '*present and future needs of the Belgian Refugees in Sevenoaks*'. Swanzy noted that:

> *Were it not for the brave resistance of the countrymen of these exiles France would probably now be completely over-run by the common enemy and the prospects of the Allies very different to what they are to-day. Try to imagine what we would feel, if, like*

Belgian refugees arrived in Sevenoaks from October 1914 onwards

these people, we were fugitives with no means of livelihood for the future. In most cases they have the terrible certainty that their homes are wrecked and they stand stripped of practically everything.

We cannot exploit the sorrows of our guests. They are here in our midst, representative of every class, members of the aristocracy, tradesmen, artisans and country people. All alike in having lost everything.

The paper also recorded the number of wounded Belgian servicemen who had arrived in Sevenoaks and the surrounding district, noting that '*some of them are really in an awful state of depression, through the loss of the greater part of their families and homes*'.

Belgian soldiers were accommodated at the local VAD hospitals, including Cornwall Hall and St John's Hall and the names of many were listed. Thanks to the Cornwall Hall archive of photographs kept by the hospital commandant Kathleen Mansfield, we know what some of these men looked like. Although a handful were named in the albums, no surname was given.

According to the *Chronicle*:

At the Cornwall Hall, one soldier was of a regiment which went out 1,400 strong and got cut up by the Germans, only 300 managing to get back to the Belgian lines. He was one of the 300, and he tells how he went over the German trenches in which it was estimated there lay between nine and ten thousand dead Germans. Another tells of how he fell into German hands but managed to escape. He had a terrible wound in his hip and a broken arm.

At St John's Hall, there were 33 Belgian patients under the commandant, (Bridget) Aurea Lambarde.

The *Chronicle* again:

The patients at this excellent hospital are all Belgians and, in spite of their great troubles, they can be heard happily singing to the tune of a gramophone. Some of them are playing cards, while others eagerly scan the contents of a French journal. The nurses... are doing excellent work, and are very grateful for all the gifts that have been sent, but we understand that all types of dried grocery and perhaps meat would be most acceptable. At this hospital it has been necessary for three operations to be performed, but the patients are progressing favourably.

The paper also carried a story of how one young Belgian soldier had not seen his brother since the start of the war and had thought him missing or injured, but discovered that he was also in Sevenoaks and was able to be reunited with him.

The generosity of the people of Sevenoaks even came from abroad. Bessie Styles, a young woman formerly of Seal near Sevenoaks who had emigrated to America wrote to Reverend Thompson, the vicar of St Mary, Kippington, asking for him to publicise the fact that together with her sister, Florence, she had collected £9 10s 4d from American donors, including one German who undertook to aid her collection. She asked that the generosity of her donors be publicised locally to reassure them that funds raised had reached the intended recipients and

**Wounded Belgian refugees were sent to local hospitals
while women and children were taken in by local residents**

so the Rev Thompson had her letter published in the *Chronicle* in December 1914.

A few weeks earlier the *Chronicle* sent an undercover reporter to chat informally to some of the wounded soldiers and refugees, who, he noted, had begun to have *'picked up quite a serviceable smattering of English and are now able to make themselves understood'.*

Taking into account the many fundraising events, appeals for food and clothing, all of which were well responded to by local people, the paper concluded:

> *Neither in the hospitals nor in the circles of private families throughout the land do we believe that the brave Belgians are being better treated than here in our own town.*

This certainly seemed to echo the sentiments of many of the new Belgian residents. On Christmas Day 1914 at the Cornwall Hall hospital, Dr Mansfield (medical officer and husband of the commandant) was presented with a framed picture by the Belgian soldiers, which had been drawn by one of the patients, George Dubois. Mrs Mansfield received a small silver stamp box and Mr Fred Keisen addressed the assembled, first in French, then English:

> *For the first time in our lives and in consequence of the grave events which are taking place at the present moment in our beloved country, we are on this holy day which commemorates the birth of our Saviour, far from our homes and families. Although this festival has not in Belgium the significance which characterises it in England, it is for us a day of great joy, for we are always at this season of the year in the bosom of our*

family. Our grief is great but great is your kindness, for it is in these cruel moments that you have done for us all that was humanly possible to soften our exile, and we thank you very sincerely.

Belgian refugees remained in the town for the duration of the war. They were found homes, supported with food and clothing, helped, where possible, into employment and the people of Sevenoaks maintained the generosity of spirit and fundraising that had welcomed the very first arrivals.

In July 1916 the Sevenoaks Belgian Refugees' Fund (which had been set up to coordinate relief) published its regular report. Since its foundation, the Fund had *'entirely supported or partially assisted over 80 persons'* – and individuals had been assisted in a variety of ways, including one disabled soldier, crippled with rheumatism for whom electrical baths had been prescribed. The man had been sent, together with his young family, to Tunbridge Wells to receive this treatment for two months, in the hope that he would in future be able to work as a chauffeur.

There were some discordant notes. The same report noted King Albert's request that his countrymen should be found employment rather than forced onto charity and the Fund recorded that:

...we have attempted to comply with His Majesty's request. In this, to our great regret, we have found ourselves hampered by the refusal of several Sevenoaks workmen to permit a Belgian among them.

In general, the evidence points to the respect and welcome that Belgian refugees received in Sevenoaks. As ever, news was anxiously awaited of local men serving with the forces and one report from a local soldier highlighted the reciprocal nature of care between the two nations. The *Chronicle* reported that Percy Ellman, nephew of local resident, Alfred Ellman, had written home to say:

My battery was gassed and we lost temporarily a 47 gun. I got lost after the 'scrap' for two days but I found a real good Belgian Samaritan, who gave me rest and food and told me he was only returning the kindness shown to Belgian refugees in England.

Support for the refugees in the town continued unabated until the Armistice. The *Chronicle* reported that many Belgians joined with townspeople in services at the Catholic church to mark the end of the war. There is little evidence to suggest how and when the refugees and wounded servicemen left the town after the end of hostilities. Possibly some kept in touch with their host families and friends they had made.

Some Belgian soldiers and refugees married local residents. Paula Storie, daughter of Alphonse Storie Van der Abeele of Bruges, arrived in Sevenoaks as a refugee in 1914. Billeted with the family of local vet, Mr Pugh, whom she supported in his work, she married his son, Leslie, in 1918. The couple had three children Peter, Marie and Christine. Paula Pugh died in May 1930 aged only 35. Her son, Peter Storie Pugh, served as a lieutenant with 6th Battalion Royal West Kent Regiment during the Second World War. He was taken prisoner and in December 1940 was taken to Colditz, where he remained until the end of the war. Peter Storie Pugh was involved in 21 escape attempts from the infamous maximum security camp. In later life he attained the rank of colonel and became President of the Royal College of Veterinary Surgeons. When he died in 2011 aged 91, he was the last survivor of the original British intake of 17 prisoners who arrived at Colditz in 1940.

The arrival of so many refugees in the town in the early days of the conflict was perhaps a stark reminder of the reality of war and how communities are easily displaced, forced to flee with what they could carry. The people of Sevenoaks rose to the occasion, welcoming those who had fled their country and supporting them throughout their stay.

A Wartime Love Story

In the churchyard at St Nicholas in the heart of Sevenoaks, there is a family grave, which bears witness to a remarkable love story between a Sevenoaks woman, Rosina Caplen, and a Belgian soldier.

The memorial to the Caplen family has now fallen into disrepair but it is still just possible to read the inscriptions to Frederick and Rosina Caplen and their two children, Frederick and Rosina. One side of the memorial includes the following inscription:

> *Also in loving memory of my dear husband,*
> *Sergeant Emile Leonard de Coster,*
> *22ⁿᵈ Infantry Belgium Army,*
> *killed about 9ᵗʰ August 1919, somewhere in Germany aged 35 years*
> *No one knows how I miss him*
> *No one knows how he died*
> *No one knows how he suffered*
> *No one knows where he lies*

This inscription was the clue to a love story and a tale of one woman's passion and determination to find out what happened to her husband.

Frederick Caplen was born in Worthing, Sussex, in 1855 and married Rosina Jane Gunn (1857-1926) in 1880. Frederick and Rosina had two children, Frederick Nathaniel (1887-1920) and Rosina Jane (1882-1948) and the 1911 census shows the family now living in Sevenoaks High Street, with Frederick senior working as a confectioner and his two children running their own hairdressing business.

Emil de Coster (spellings of his first name vary) arrived, wounded or otherwise, during 1914. He was recorded in the *Sevenoaks Chronicle* as being a patient at the St John's VAD Hospital in October 1914. It is likely that he met Rosina, a talented singer and performer, during a concert at the hospital or elsewhere in the town. The couple married early in 1917. Emil is not mentioned again until a brief report of his death by drowning in 1919. A full account of the story does not appear until three years later in an article in the *Sevenoaks Chronicle* on 15th September 1922.

Entitled *Sevenoaks Woman's Search for Her Husband's Grave*, the article describes how Rosina, now Madame de Coster, had searched for three years for the grave of her husband, who had died while he was serving with the Army of Occupation in Germany.

According to the paper, after years of *'unavailing inquiries'* as to the circumstances of her husband Emil's death and burial place, Rosina travelled to Brussels to make inquiries in person. At Brussels she was able to trace and meet one of the officers of her late husband's regiment who told her the full story of his death. He told her that:

Just after dinner, Sergeant de Coster went with others to the soldiers' bathing pond. He had not been long in the water when he was seized with cramp. His comrades rescued him from the water and a doctor was called, but life was extinct. They buried him with full military honours in a pretty little churchyard at Rheinberg.

Having learnt this, the intrepid Rosina set off for Rheinberg, some 400 miles across the frontier; she reached Cologne, where her impression was that *'the British soldier rules'*. In her words *'The Germans are afraid of them'*. According to the paper:

Everything she found to be fearfully expensive to the Germans, and the effect of the downfall of the Mark (it was 8000 to the £ during her visit) is illustrated by the fact that the journey from Brussels to Cologne, 2nd class, was only 2s in English money. 'There were plenty of English people in Germany but it is difficult to bring anything out owing to the Customs'.

EVENO AKS WOMAN'S SEARCH FOR HUSBAND'S GRAVE.

FINDS IT IN GERMAN CHURCHYARD.

For the past three years Mme. de Coster, daughter of Mr. and Mrs. F. N. B. Caplen, Coniston, The Drive, Sevenoaks, has conducted an untiring search for the grave of her husband, Sergt. Emile de Coster, of the Belgian Army, whose death occurred some three years ago while with the Army of Occupation in Germany. The details furnished at the time were very meagre.

Wearied of the unavailing inquiries by correspondence, Mme. de Coster took on herself the journey to the Continent to discover, if she could, the whereabouts of her husband's grave, and visit it.

She commenced her search at Brussels, and after many inquiries, succeeded in locating one of the officers of her late husband's regiment. This officer told her the full story of how Sergt. de Coster met his death.

How the *Chronicle* reported Rosina's search

Following a further 12 hours train journey, Rosina arrived at Rheinberg and was able to visit her husband's grave. There she met a German woman who had witnessed the funeral and was able to give more detail on his death and burial.

The paper concluded that Rosina's one desire was to have her husband's body returned to Sevenoaks for reburial and that she was making an appeal to the Belgian War Office for this. Failing that, she wished her husband's body to be returned for burial in his home town.

Rosina's efforts were ultimately successful as Emil's body was exhumed on 1ˢᵗ June 1923 and removed to his home town of Belsele for reburial.

Some years later in January 1931, the *Sevenoaks Chronicle* reported that Madame de Coster was presented to Baron and Baroness Moschier the Belgian Ambassador and his wife, at a party given by the Society des Invalides at the Earl Haig Memorial Hall, Fulham, in memory of the Belgian soldiers who fell during the Great War. Later that year, in the November, as the only known widow of a Belgian serviceman in England, Rosina de Coster laid a wreath at the Cenotaph in Whitehall on behalf of the Belgian Federation.

Little is known about Emil's life before the war. He was born on 25ᵗʰ January 1886 in Belsele, St Niklaas, to Charles Louis August de Coster, an agricultural worker, and his wife Francoise. It is possible that Emil had two brothers, Gabriel, born 1887, and Leo Frans, born 1889, and the family, at least around 1919, were living at Groenstraat 6, Belsele.

His widow, Rosina, continued to live in Sevenoaks and, as a singer and performer, took part in many local productions and events. She lived on at her home *'Coniston'* on The Drive, Sevenoaks, until 1948, when she was buried in the family grave at St Nicholas. For many years, Rosina posted an In Memoriam notice in the *Sevenoaks Chronicle* in remembrance of her husband on the anniversary of his death.

Rosina and Emil did not have children and neither did her brother, Frederick. It is possible that Emil's brothers did have children and that there are descendents today who might one day be able to provide more information on this story of a couple brought together by the war and Rosina's remarkable determination to discover what had happened to her husband and to ensure that he was remembered in Sevenoaks and reburied in the place of his birth.

VAD Hospitals and Nursing in Sevenoaks

The Voluntary Aid Detachment, commonly known as VAD, was founded in 1909 to fill the gaps in Territorial medical services. Male and female detachments were set up and would meet regularly. Training in first aid and nursing was provided to the volunteers, many of whom were unlikely to have had previous nursing experience. There were several VAD hospitals in and around the Sevenoaks area during the war. Led and staffed by women, mostly

VAD nurses and staff at the Cornwall Hall hospital

from the middle and upper classes. Several albums and records of the local hospitals survive, especially those of the Cornwall Hall hospital, where Kathleen Mansfield and her husband were in charge, and of the Wildernesse Hospital.

The local VAD hospitals included Kent 56, covering the Club Hall and St John's Hall run until summer 1915 by (Bridget) Aurea Lambarde, daughter of the well-known Lambarde family of Bradbourne Hall and Kent 76, covering Cornwall Hall and the Kippington Parish Room, initially run by Katie Hilder. Kent 56 had been established by Vita Sackville West and Dr John Sterry. Vita resigned in late 1913 but became the Honorary Commandant. The Hon. Violet

Staff and patients at Cornwall Hall

Nurses & patients at the Cornwall Hall hospital

Mills was in charge at the hospital set up in the stable block on her father's Wildernesse estate. Two hospitals were also established in Chipstead, at the Mission Hall and at Chipstead Place. The hospitals relied on donations and fundraising. Appeals for financial gifts as well as goods and produce were made throughout the war, to supplement the government funding.

Shortly after Britain declared war, an ambulance brigade for Sevenoaks was established with an initial 50 volunteers attending the first meeting, when practical examples of stretcher bearing were given. Dr Mansfield, medical officer at the Cornwall Hall VAD hospital, explained the duties that would be required, and how the wounded might arrive by rail at any time and in any number, from six to a hundred. The stretcher bearers would perform a vital role and relieve the worry on the nursing staff.

Initially, soldiers staying in the town were invited to a smoking concert at the Cornwall Hall. A room had been equipped for reading and writing and another as a games room with a small billiard table, as well as a bagatelle table and games such as chess, draughts, and dominoes. Tea and refreshments were provided every evening from 8 to 9 and entertainments were held on Friday evenings. A ward was made available for the men of the Royal West Kent Territorials. Very shortly Belgian refugees and the first wounded arrived.

The first wounded men to arrive from the Front, carried entirely in private cars donated for the purpose, reached Sevenoaks on 14th October 1914. The first large direct convoy of 146 cases arrived on 14th March 1915. The biggest direct convoy to be received in the town was the 160 wounded men that arrived on 22nd June 1916, who were then allocated to the various local hospitals by the VAD Transport Officer, De Barri Crawshay, aided by his son, Lionel. After the war, it was calculated that 13,485 sick and wounded had been cared for in the VAD hospitals in the Sevenoaks area (including 2,916 at Cornwall Hall; 2,171 at St John's Hall and 1,510 at Wildernesse). Casualties arrived in the town via Sevenoaks station until the later stages of the war when this was transferred to Otford, where the men could be more easily transported to the local hospitals.

Mrs Beatrice Anckorn of Dunton Green received a message early one morning to say she was needed at the Chipstead Mission Hall urgently. She later told the *Sevenoaks Chronicle:*

I rushed to Martin's in Dunton Green, bought a uniform, borrowed a governess cart and drove to Chipstead. There I helped to scrub the floors and put up beds. We were hardly ready when the first Belgians began to arrive. They had walked from the station and were covered in blood, filthy bedraggled and unshaven. We gave them soup and bundled them into beds after cleaning their wounds.

A report in the *Kent Messenger* in October 1914 noted that 53 wounded soldiers were being nursed in Chipstead village, sixteen of whom were English. They came mainly from the Bedford, Dorset and Cornwall regiments and had been through several battles, including Mons. According to the paper, when questioned on the subject of German atrocities, they all stated that:

…the allegations were correct. In Belgium, women had sent their children on, and had faced the rifle fire in order to save them. The men also alleged that they had seen women with their hands cut off. On several occasions our Tommies had gone without food for days because of having given all their rations to the starving. The soldiers seem confident that in the long run we shall beat the Germans, and beat them easily. We draw them on with a bit of sweetmeat, and then let them have it.

Kathleen Mansfield was commandant at the Cornwall Hall hospital on The Drive, Sevenoaks. Born Kathleen Lilian Clark in October 1885 in Portadown, she attended Sidcot Quaker school and went on to train as a nurse at Almondsbury Memorial Hospital, north of Bristol. In 1910, she married Dr Percy Mansfield, a family doctor in Sevenoaks and they went on to have four children.

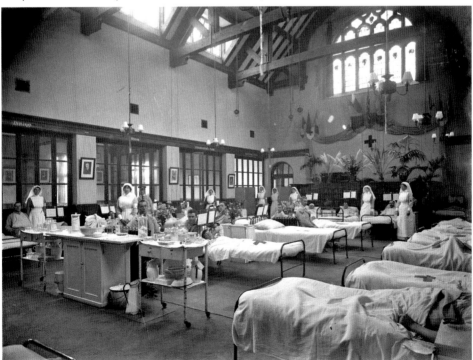

The ward at the Cornwall Hall hospital

Kathleen Mansfield joined the VAD in 1912 and soon held the post of lady superintendent. When a VAD hospital was set up at Cornwall Hall near where the couple lived, Kathleen joined, and became the commandant after the resignation of Katie Hilder in November 1914. Kathleen's husband, Percy, was the medical officer.

Kathleen and her husband served for the majority of the war, tireless in their work of caring for the refugees and wounded servicemen that arrived. Dr Mansfield was called up to serve with the Royal Army Medical Corps in 1917 and so his wife stepped down from her duties temporarily. Kathleen kept meticulous records, including photographs and letters from the servicemen, with names and service numbers carefully inscribed. The archive also includes photos of the nursing staff, who were mainly drawn from the local upper and middle class families of the town, as well as photos of sports days, fancy dress parades and festive celebrations. This precious material includes the glowing testimony of many of their former charges now returned to the Front and recalling the care and comfort that they had received, speaks of the dedication and compassion of the commandant and her nursing team. Kathleen was awarded the Royal Red Cross in 1917 in recognition of her service. She died in 1962, having survived her husband by twelve years.

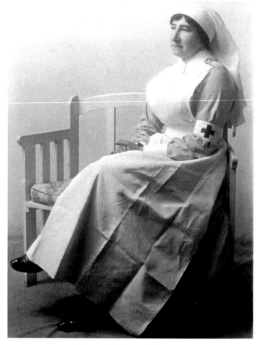

Emma Snow Crump

Emma Snow Crump worked at Cornwall Hall for the duration of the war. She was born in 1873 in Devon and the 1901 census for Wales shows her working at the Monmouthshire Lunatic Asylum. Ten years later, the 1911 census showed Emma employed as a nurse at Sevenoaks workhouse in Sundridge. Emma Crump joined the staff at Cornwall Hall as a night nurse in October 1914, becoming sister in 1915, matron in 1918 and matron in sole charge, 1919. According to her records, she was paid 30s per week in 1914. By 1919 this had increased to £2 per week. Emma married in 1926 and lived on until 1952.

**Drawing of May Benson by Fred Brooke of
Nottinghamshire, in her autograph book**

May Benson was born in 1892 in France, the daughter of Alfred Edward Benson (1863-1899) and his wife, Dora Sophia Turner (1862-1896). The 1911 census shows that May had moved to England and was living with her mother's sister, Alice Andrews, and her husband, Henry, at *The Limes*, Hollingbourne, Kent. All of the family are shown as having 'private means'.

Records of the Red Cross show that May was living at 9, Granville Road, Sevenoaks, when she was taken on as a nurse probationer in March 1917 at the Cornwall Hall. May worked part-time on night duty until March 1918. Throughout her time she kept an album, given to her by her Aunt Alice, which she used to ask wounded servicemen, including some Belgians, to sign. Many of the men wrote or sketched in May's book, often giving their regiment and other details, making it an invaluable source for further research. May Benson married Arthur Clarke and lived until 1983 when she died, aged 91, in York.

Men like Fred Pearce (son of Fred Pearce, a well-known local fishmonger) also worked at Cornwall Hall. Pearce later made a successful application to work at the Royal Victoria Hospital, Netley, for which Kathleen Mansfield wrote a letter of recommendation in December 1916. Fred Pearce worked at Netley from January 1917 until February 1919. Of his three brothers, Charlie, was in the Loyal North Lancashire regiment; John served with the Army Service Corps and Albert saw active service with the West Kent Yeomanry and was wounded at Gallipoli.

Throughout the war, the staff of the local VAD hospitals cared for the thousands of injured servicemen that passed through their doors (the last wounded man arrived in Sevenoaks as late as 28th April 1919). Supported by local residents and businesses, the hospitals benefitted from fundraising drives, entertainments and other donations. Patients at St John's Hall VAD were entertained by a young Welshman, David Ivor Davies, who lived in a Romany caravan in the grounds of his mother's home at Biggin Hill. Davies sang a song he had recently composed, *'Keep the Homes Fires Burning'*, which became a classic of the war. He later took his mother's maiden name as his surname and restyled himself as Ivor Novello.

A Grateful Patient: Captain Eric Wilkinson MC

Amongst the archive material kept by Kathleen Mansfield at Cornwall Hall, is a carefully preserved three page letter, written entirely in verse and signed Eric F Wilkinson. Wilkinson is also the subject of a newspaper article on the following page of the scrapbook.

He was Captain Eric Fitzwalter Wilkinson who served with A Company of 8th Battalion West Yorkshire Regiment (Leeds Rifles). Wilkinson was born in 1891 and was educated at Dorchester and then Ilkley Grammar School. He took an engineering course at Leeds University and later became a Master at Ilkley Grammar School. Before the war he wrote poetry for the school magazine and he continued to write during his time in the army, which he joined in 1915. Some of his poetry was published and well received during the war in the collection *Sunrise Dreams and other poems*, which includes the poems *Cornwall Hall* and *My Nurse*, which refer to his time at the eponymous hospital in Sevenoaks.

While serving as a lieutenant with the Leeds Rifles, he won the Military Cross in July 1915, according to the citation, *'Near St Julien, he assisted to carry a wounded soldier for a distance of 120 yards into cover under circumstances of great difficulty and danger'*. He was also twice mentioned in despatches.

He was wounded in winter 1915, during a bayonet attack and was also later gassed. He was injured in July 1916 during the battle of the Somme and appears to have spent some time in hospital at Chatham before arriving at Cornwall Hall. Later that year, Wilkinson wrote this letter (on 24th November 1916), to Kathleen Mansfield:

> *Dear Commandant*
>
> *I'm sitting in a room,*
> *The candle lighted, - all the rest in gloom.*
> *Two candles, guttering from bottle necks,*
> *Throw light, and shadow, onto tattered wrecks*
> *Of walls and windows, broken chairs and beds,*
> *(Where French civilians used to lay their heads)*
> *- For you, must know, this used to be the home,*
> *Of tillers of the clayey Picard loam.*
> *The place was shelled to blazes by the Bosch,*
> *- I'm sitting on a tub to write this tosche-.*
> *And so we make our mess, and wake, and sleep*

Eric Fitzwater Wilkinson (1891-1917)

In ruined rooms where small rats crawl and creep
And great rats run, and leap, and gnaw anything
And all around, the desolation clings.
Yet we can sleep the night through, without fear:
No conscious sentries need be watchful here:
A mile behind the line, we're 'Out on Rest',
And, when we go to bed, may get undressed,
Each day we take our men to dig and toil
To clear the trenches of the shell-blown soil
That now is heavy mud: each night, again
Return to billets, that keep out the rain,
To sleep; or, if our work is done at night,
- It sometimes is, - Sleep through the hours of light.
Our own guns all around us roar and bay,
And Bosche shells, meant for them, come round our way
But, for six days, the Front line, and its cares,
Night-watches, bullets, mortars, bombs and flares,
Are off our minds, and we can sit and write
To those we've often thought of in the night;
Or in that long slow hour, when laggard dawn

Peers through a drenching mist on fields forlorn,
Full often, in those hours, a vision seemed
To float before my eyes, or else I dreamed:
I saw the little hospital, and those, -
The memory of whose kindness only grows
With lapse of time; and oftentimes I swore
To write and tell the gratitude I bore.
So, Commandant, before I go to bed,
I call down blessings on your kindly head,
Please give the doc my love, and matron too,
And Sister Crump, and Flo, and all I knew.
And when the work seems hard, and old Fort Pitt,
Sends bounders round, whose manners aren't a bit,
What colonels manners should be, far from it,
Just say 'Our Patients' gratitude is ours, -
'What care we for the manners of the Powers
'That Be', and carry on the same old way.
So when I get a 'blighty' some great day
I can return to Seven Oaks and be
Once more a lucky patient in ward III
Believe me to remain, - till time is done

Yours gratefully - Eric F Wilkinson.

The author of the newspaper article also in the Cornwall Hall archive, identifies himself as Eric Wilkinson's uncle. He was inspired to write by overhearing a chance remark which suggested that every soldier at the Front would gladly lose a limb, so as to return home with a 'Blighty'. The author feels moved to detail the true nature of men like his nephew who had, by this time, been killed at Passchendaele in 1917, as an answer to this slur:

He was my sister's son. When war broke out, he was a master in a Wharfedale gram-
mar-school but a boy all the same, though twenty-three years old. By virtue of peace-
time-training with the O.T.C. he got an immediate commission in the West Yorkshire
Regiment (Leeds Rifles) and went to France early in 1915. All through the winter of
1915-16 he was in the nameable trenches in front of Ypres, nothing more serious befall-
ing him than a bayonet wound and a partial asphyxiation by poison-gas.

His part in the great battle of July 1 1916 was the abortive attack on the strong-
hold of Thiepval. 'During the night' he wrote to me 'I went up to support some men of
another division in a trench we had taken and found it had been recaptured. I went
in with twelve men and said 'Hullo!' to the first person I met, who promptly lobbed
a bomb at me. Greatly scandalised, I said 'English, you thundering fool!' whereas
he and divers unruly other companions did pelt us with bombs. Five of us got away,
three wounded'. The horrid wound that fell to his share brought him back to Blighty.
Writing from a hospital at Chatham he said 'So far, we have abstracted one piece of

bomb-casing and half a tunic but we suspect the presence of a pair of trousers as I came back the night it happened practically without, and they seem to have gone somewhere'.

Convalescent, he went to Cornwall Hall, in Kent. … it abides in the minds of many men and many mothers of men on a high place and in a strong light of grateful memory. The Boy paid his tribute in a nurse's album

> *A little hospital in Kent*
> *As, in a vision I shall see*
> *Where lucky men are sometimes sent,*
> *And kind eyes smile encouragement,*
> *And once they smiled on me*
> *And proud and strong my heart shall be*
> *That I am fit to strike a blow*
> *To keep our English women free –*
> *Like those who did so much for me*
> *A little while ago.*

Last summer (1917) he was gassed:

'The Bosche have been trying a new gas on us and I don't think much of it'. But he was blind for three days and his sight permanently affected.

On Oct 9 last, leading the first wave of attack on some part of the Passchendaele Ridge, he fell. His attitude toward death was summed up in some lines he had written:

> *Mourn not for me too sadly; I have been*
> *For months of an exalted life, a King,*
> *Peer for these months of those whose graves grow green*
> *Where're the borders of our empire fling*
> *Their mighty arms. And if the crown is death,*
> *Death while I'm fighting for my home and King,*
> *Thank God! The son who drew from you his breath*
> *To death could bring*
> *A not entirely worthless sacrifice,*
> *Because of those brief months when life meant more*
> *Than selfish pleasures. Grudge not then the price*
> *But say, 'Our country in the storm of war*
> *Has found him fit to fight and die for her.'*
> *And lift your heads in pride for evermore.*
> *but when the leaves the evening breezes stir*
> *Close not the door.*
> *But listen to the wind that hurries by,*
> *To all the Song of Life for tones you knew;*
> *For in the voice of birds, the scent of flowers,*
> *The evening silence and the falling dew,*
> *Through every throbbing pulse of Nature's powers*

I'll speak to you

And again:

> *The mother who sent him bowed her head*
> *And wept for the lad she bore;*
> *Yet never she grudged her sacred dead,*
> *For her country's need was sore*
> *'He died for his King and the Right',*
> *She said,*
> *'And no man could do more'*

Mutiny at Etaples

Eric Wilkinson was also involved in one of the war's more controversial events, the mutiny at Etaples. Etaples was a training camp for veterans of the frontline, providing refresher training. Criticism was often made of the harsh regime at the infamous 'Bullring' and of the staff and officers, especially the NCOs, and their alleged lack of experience at the Front.

During the disturbances at Etaples, Corporal Jesse Robert Short of 24th Battalion North-umberland Fusiliers, was accused of inciting men to lay down their arms and attack one of their officers; this was Eric Wilkinson. Short had spent two years at the Front, been wounded and later sent to Etaples. He did not challenge Wilkinson's account of the incident, which was confirmed by his second in command. According to the records of Short's court martial, on 11th September 1917, Wilkinson's evidence stated:

> *On the afternoon of the 11th instant, I was in charge of a Picquet of 150 armed and 50 unarmed men on the Bridge over the River Canche leading from Etaples to Paris-Plage. At about 9.15 pm about 80 men marched towards the Bridge from Etaples, some of them armed with sticks and notice boards. The Picquet failed to stop these men from crossing the Bridge. The accused detached himself from this party and while I was addressing my Picquet and remonstrating with them for failing to stand-fast. The accused started haranguing them. Referring to me he said 'you want to put a rope round that bugger's neck tie a stone to it and throw him into the River', and he told the men that they should not listen to me. Within a few minutes I was able to get the accused arrested.*

Jesse Short was tried and sentenced to death. This was confirmed by Sir Douglas Haig on 30th September. The execution was carried out on 4th October 1917.

Wilkinson's war record and his poetry shows how far he was from being the caricature of an officer who sought an easy life well behind the lines nor an unrelenting disciplinarian. He died only four days after Corporal Short's execution, on 9th October, having been moved on from Etaples to rejoin his unit in the Ypres salient as it prepared for an attack on the Pass-chendaele Ridge. On a morning filled with heavy rain, the Leeds Rifles suffered heavy losses in the Battle of Poelcappelle

'Amid the sea of mud he became separated from his men and was last seen making single-handed for the enemy lines'.

Captain Eric Wilkinson is remembered at the Tyne Cot memorial to the missing.

~

Part Three

ACTIVE SERVICE

Action at Sea

In the early weeks of the war, a number of men from Sevenoaks who were by then in training or already on active service, wrote to the *Sevenoaks Chronicle* with tales of their exploits. One of the first to do so was Thomas Porter. Thomas was born in Sevenoaks in 1891, the son of Thomas Porter and his wife, Ellen. The 1911 census showed Thomas as aged 24, living at 13, Redman Place, High Street, Sevenoaks, with his parents and four of his siblings.

Thomas's letters are accounts of his time as a stoker on the *Arethusa* during the Battle of Heligoland Bight, the first naval battle of the war, which was fought on the 28th August 1914.

Thomas had joined the Royal Navy on 6th August 1909, for the usual period of twelve years. At the time of his joining up he was working as a plumber and his papers show that he was nearly 5'4 tall, with a fresh complexion, brown eyes and hair. Thomas served on a number of ships before joining the *Arethusa*. From 1909 he was part of the crew of nine ships including the *Pembroke, Agamenon*, and *Blenheim*. He was promoted acting stoker while still with the *Arethusa* in January 1915 but left the ship that March and continued to serve with the Navy until October 1919 when, as leading stoker, he was invalided out of the service with his character having been 'Very Good' throughout.

Thomas wrote two letters that were published, the first to his mother, the second to the *Sevenoaks Chronicle*. He tries to strike a reassuring tone in the letter to his mother, which was published in the paper on 4th September:

Don't worry over me as I am as safe as 'houses'. Since I said goodbye to Dad and the boys, I have been in the thick of the war and thank God for that. He has spared me to come back. We were in the great battle of Heligoland and I am sorry to say we have eleven killed and two wounded. We were engaged in the battle for six hours and our ship sunk four German cruisers, eight submarines and two torpedo destroyers. You talk about the charge of the Light Brigade, it was not in it. Now no more. We had a very rough time so now I will close. I have a lot to tell you when I write again, so goodbye, I remain, your loving son, Tom.

The second letter was published the following week on 11th September. Billed as the *Full Story of the Arethusa by a Sevenoaks 'Jack Tar'*.

This is an account of the great battle of Heligoland. I am just writing as I was an eye witness. It was a sight I shall never forget. We had only been in commission a week. We left on the Thursday from Harwich to try and decoy the skulkers out into the North Sea.

My captain told us the night before we went into action that we were going to have a rub at them sometime next morning. We were steaming all night long without lights, which was a very dangerous job, as there were forty-seven destroyers of the British and two 2nd class cruisers about – the Arethusa *and HMS Fearless. Well, all went well until about 7 o'clock next morning, and then we were at it.*

There was a black fog all around us, but we were not more than three miles off the big forts of Heligoland, and we could see the German destroyers coming to meet us. But we had no idea we were going to meet cruisers. We opened fire on them and of course they retaliated and we had not been in action more than 20 minutes when we sunk one of their destroyers. Yes! Our boats peppered it into them. Then all of a sudden we saw a big cruiser coming towards us, so of course we had to do our best. I had just come off watch, and the fog was still very black, and as I came on deck a terrible sight I saw. Dead and wounded all around me, and the shells of the Germans still bursting over our heads. But we had to stick it. I did my best. I gave a hand with the wounded but I could not see a stretcher, and so I picked up a piece of old canvas, carried two poor chaps to sick bay in it, and back I came.

We came out of action and we had not been out about half an hour when our skipper sighted another two cruisers of the enemy, so of course we had to face the music once more. And this time we all thought it was all up with us, as we were badly damaged. We had our gunners shot away from their guns like nine-pins, and others came up to take their places and then we had four guns out of action, but we had two or three to carry on with, as we meant to fight until the last. Then all of a sudden we sighted the cruisers and battle cruisers of our own Fleet coming to our assistance. It was a Godsend, because we were hit badly below the waterline. We could only steam 20 knots then, as our engines had nearly been put out of action, and afterwards we had to be towed home to Bonny England by the cruiser Hague, and when we got to Sheerness we did get a 'chuck-up' by the lads on the battleships.

Mr Churchill came aboard and had a look over our ship to see the damage and to look at our poor lads who had fallen in the battle. After all we went through, it was a marvel to come out of it all. And last of all I must tell you that our captain told us that we had all done our duty and the next time we went in action he hoped we would put our trust in him as he had put his trust in us. We are going to have another out later on to see if we can make some more of them come out and go under.

This short but detailed piece was the first account of any Sevenoaks man who had experienced combat to be published and read by local people.

Thomas's brothers were also on active service. On 21st September 1917, in its regular 'Our Boys' column, George Porter was mentioned as a sapper in the Royal Engineers home on leave from his current base at Canterbury. According to the brief article, George's brother Ernest was serving with the Kent Cyclists while Tom was remembered as being *'for some time on board the* Arethusa *when she did saucy things in the North Sea'.*

All of the Porter brothers appear to have survived the war but there was one wartime casualty in the family with the death of their sister, Clarice May Cross née Porter (1892-1918). In its account of her burial, the *Chronicle* reported that Clarice had died of blood poisoning in hospital in Folkestone. Her obituary noted briefly that Clarice had worked in a munitions factory during the war *'and there contracted the disease of which she died'.* Clarice was buried in the cemetery at St Nicholas, her coffin carried by her brother Tom and other serving soldiers and sailors. She left behind her husband, Clarence, and baby daughter, Clarice, who was just a few weeks old.

Another of Thomas's sisters, Elsie Nellie (1886-1975) married Charlie Draper (see page 88).

Cedric Gordon's War

Of the four Gordon brothers who fought in the First World War, two are remembered on the Sevenoaks War Memorial. Donald Jervis Gordon, a second lieutenant in the 8th Battalion Border Regiment, was the first to be killed. He died on the third day of the battle of the Somme in July 1916.

His younger brother, Bernard Vernon Gordon, was killed later that year in December 1916, in a flying accident in Northumberland whilst serving with the Royal Flying Corps (see page 81).

The remaining brothers who fought were Thomas Milford Gordon – a second lieutenant in the Royal Engineers, and Cedric Foskett Gordon. Another brother, (Edward) Basil, could not enlist owing to his health and was a master at Lancing College, where he helped run the Officer Training Corps.

Cedric lived to the ripe old age of 89, dying in Sevenoaks in 1979 (he was buried in the churchyard at Kemsing, having lived in the village with his brother and sister in his later years). Like his brothers, Donald and Basil, he was educated at Lancing College, where he excelled in sports. In 1910, he was commissioned into the North Staffordshire Regiment. He was sent to France in September 1914 and was awarded the Military Cross (*London Gazette*, 16th February 1915) for the intelligence he was able to obtain on German deployment, an experience he recounted in a letter home. Cedric was a prolific letter writer and many of his letters to his family survive, including this, which was written on 24th September after his escapade. It was published anonymously in *The Times* on 10th October 1914.

Letter to darlingest Mother,

We have started fighting. The Battle we are in has been going on for days, I think 8 or 9. I believe the main body of the enemy are now on the retreat, and I expect we shall soon be on the track following them up. I hope we shall get a decisive victory soon. Two days ago we arrived here, a town under shell fire, and I was at once sent on (it was about 11pm and very dark) to go to the enemy's trenches with three scouts to see if they were still there. It was a decidedly dangerous job. The General sent me out. I went about 300 yards in front of my scouts. It was a pretty jumpy job. The enemy's trenches were about 950 yds from ours. I paced about 850 yds and then got down on my hands and knees and crept on for some way expecting every moment to run into a German trench. It was pretty black and I could only see a few yards in front of me. I crawled along for some way but didn't come across anything. I had a loaded revolver and a map with me. Every now and then I came across a dead German, rather creepy.

Well I couldn't think why I had not struck the trenches so I went off to my left a bit as I thought I might have got too far off to my right. After I had wandered about for some time I got quite flummoxed and didn't know where I was. The stars had gone in and I was pretty well lost in the middle of this big open plateau, expecting every moment to run into a German trench. After a bit I heard some people talking. I approached cautiously and heard that they were talking German so I sheered off again.

Cedric Foskett Gordon

After wandering about for a considerable time I heard some carts driving up the road. I approached with caution. There were four of them; I let the three leading ones go by and stepped out to the fourth, and put my revolver to the driver's head and told him to halt. By Jove, the poor fellow was terrified. He put his arm in front of his face and squealed. I hadn't the heart to shoot him, it would have been too much like murder. I let him go past and had a couple of rounds at his cart when he was past. He fairly let his horses have it, and went off at a gallop. The last I saw of him he was driving like a madman across country, I don't know what became of him. Well I thought it was about time to be moving as I didn't wish anyone to come along and find me so I went off in the opposite direction, I was completely lost and it was pretty dark. I wandered about and tried to find my track but I could not manage it.

Suddenly I saw about a foot in front of me a trench full of men sitting down with their backs towards me. I was a bit surprised and was not sure whether they were our fellows or not. I said 'Hello', the man, I think it was an officer, who was nearest me turned round and said 'Es ist ein Englander' or words to that effect. I didn't wait to say good morning but shifted for all I was worth. I was followed by a regular tornado of bullets, I ran about 250 yds and then I came across a small trench into which I hopped. After I had been there about a minute I thought it was about time to be off so I got up and began to run again. I hadn't been above ten yards when people began to shoot at me from all sides. I thought things were getting past a joke so, seeing a hole just to my right, I fell headlong into it, being in a bit of a hurry.

It was now getting light and I could see it was hopeless trying to get on again, so I reconciled myself to the prospect of staying the day there, and trying to get on under cover of darkness next night. I discovered that the hole I was in was made by one of the enemy's big shells striking the ground. The men refer to this gun of the German's as 'Little Willy'. I was jolly thankful to 'Little Willy' for making such a nice big hole. It was about 10 ft across and 2'6' or 3' deep at the bottom and sort of V shaped. After having cogitated for a short while I came to the conclusion that I was behind the enemy's line and must have crept through between two trenches in the dark; as I had met their transport on the road, that is what I must have done. I thought that if I just lay there I should be taken prisoner for a ship so I decided to bury myself. I set about it, my only implement being a jack-knife. In time I accomplished it. The ground was stiff clay and awfully cold and awfully heavy. I stuck it for some time and got cramp in both my legs and finally I could not stick it any longer, so I unburied myself and decided that if any Germans did come along I would lie as if I were dead, and take my luck. I was in that hole from 4 am till about 8pm at night and it was quite the worst day I have ever spent. I had nothing to do and could not even sit up. I hadn't anything to eat or drink and I thought a very doubtful chance of ever getting away – I got quite homesick! It was dreadfully lonely and being hungry did not improve things. However I kept fairly cheerful on the whole. I tried doing everything I could think of, even cutting my hair with a very blunt pair of scissors. I didn't get very far with that job! I also worked a fancy needlework for you, which I will give you when I return.

I lay on my back most of the day and listened to the shells whistling past, and watched aeroplanes. There were a good many about altogether. I peeped cautiously out of my hole. Occasionally I could see the Germans about 200 yards from where I was in their trenches. I was now in front of them, they must have been sideways on to the one I ran into. There was a poor beggar dead (a German) not very far from me. There was a hedge about 200 yards from me on the opposite side from the Germans and I decided to creep for it at dark and to try and work my way round to the village where I left the Regiment. There was a good bit of rifle fire just over me, and I could hear shooting from the direction of the hedge, but I couldn't see the bottom of it. It then struck me that our troops might be holding it. Well at dusk I shouted lustily towards the hedge that I was coming and told them not to shoot and crept forth. When I had gone some way I was advancing with my hands up and I should say that I was about 100yds from the hedge, a couple of rounds came whizzing past me. I fell down flat and crawled a bit nearer and shouted again. This time they heard me and after some parleying let me come in. I found that it was one of the Regiments in our Brigade and that our Regiment was in position on their left. By Jove I was thankful to find I was safely back. The loneliness was one of the worst parts of it. I wished I had old Bill (his dog) with me in my hole.

Well I got back to our Regiment and was greeted as one returned from the dead! It was a rather trying experience, but I am none the worse for it. We are now in the trenches. Our Regiment is occupying the front of a wood and only half of it is there at a time, the other half returning to the little village in the valley below. I was in the village last night and slept in a real bed. The first time for 6 weeks. I slept from 12.30 in the morning to 5am next day with about 3½ hrs break in the middle. I had been up for two nights with only about ½ hr sleep altogether. It was topping. We came up into the trenches again this morning. There is nothing much doing. We get shelled occasionally and there are a few snipers about, but we have hardly had a man hit. Most shrapnel wounds are not too bad. I've got a jolly little trench and cave affair to get into when they start shelling and am as safe as a house. I got up a tree this morning with a sergeant and we did a bit of sniping. I think we hit a couple but it's very hard to say. I had no luck! I expect you are glad! They found us out in the end and started potting at us. We descended mighty quickly. I am quite well and having a good time but still I shall be glad to get back again. I haven't had a letter since we left England but I think only letters posted on the 11th have reached us so far. We are really quite safe, don't be anxious dear old Mater. I thought about you and them all a good bit the other day when I was in Little Willy's hole. I do hope you are all well.

Cedric's second injury (following a wound to his foot caused by a colleague's bayonet in December 1914) was sustained in the spring of 1915. He was severely wounded in the left leg

Cedric, on left, having lost his left leg

after a successful attack on the village of L'Epinette. He was evacuated to a military hospital in Cambridge and the leg was subsequently removed above the knee.Any other man might have considered this the end of his active military career but Cedric was attached to the Royal Flying Corps and continued his wartime service as an observer and air gunner (while still a captain in the North Staffordshire Regiment). By the end of the war he had 73.43 hours in his log book. He was subsequently awarded the Croix de Guerre in 1918, was mentioned in dispatches four times and awarded the military class of the OBE in 1919.

According to one of his nephews, quoted in his obituary, Cedric was shot at during one flight with the bullet shattering his wooden leg. On landing, he was said to have found the stray bullet in his pocket and was confined to bed until the camp carpenter had made him a new leg.

Cedric (right) flew with the Royal Flying Corps for the remainder of the war

After the war, Cedric was sent to Russia with British forces to aid the White Russians in the Crimea in their fight against the Bolsheviks. He was awarded the Distinguished Flying Cross and received the Order of St Ann and the Order of St Stanislas from the Russians. After leaving Russia, his journey home was delayed by the lack of available boats, so he and a friend decided to borrow a plane to visit Jerusalem. He was forced to land in the desert and was, according to his obituary '*picked up by a band of friendly Arabs*'. He was awarded his 'Wings' as a pilot on Christmas Eve 1926 and had a foot specially made to allow him to operate the pedals.

Cedric was later based in Hong Kong as British Air Attaché for China, before returning to England and taking command of the RAF Balloon Centre. During the Second World War, he was eventually put in charge of the South East Air Training Corps and was also a member of the Home Guard.

On his retirement he returned to Lancing College where his brother, Basil, was a master. Later in life he became well known in Sevenoaks for his involvement in the local scouting movement and is still remembered fondly by all who knew him.

Cedric's cousin, Martin Gordon, remembers him:

He lived in a big house with grounds in Sevenoaks. He had big vegetable gardens, a large pig, called Mr Pig, and even a little wood on a hill. He had a little MG which he used to drive my sister and I into town with - we stood up in the boot. He never married and lived with his sister Kathleen. She affectionately called him 'Beast' and he had a similarly uncomplimentary name for her, which I can no longer remember. He was a wonderful man- we lived near London, but we drove over to visit about once a year when I was a child, and it was always one of my favourite days of the year.

To my shame, I never quizzed him about his life. All I can remember is that he was a pilot in World War I and he lost a leg. He still had the trench coat he was wearing when he was wounded, with a hole burned in it – he showed it to me. He said he also fought in Russia after the war for the RAF. One of the things he told me was that when he was in Russia, he was shot down and had to walk through the snow back to base. I have recently been able to check the facts, and this is what actually happened:

On 23rd December 1919 the plane he was in was hit and they had to make a forced landing behind enemy lines. He and the pilot burned the plane and set off walking through the winter snow. You can imagine how cold it was, Christmas time in Russia! And they didn't get back to base until the next day. I can't imagine how he did that with one leg.

Throughout his life, Cedric was a popular figure. Generous and thoughtful with children, whom he treated as intelligent adults, he lives on in the memories of those whom he befriended. As far from Sevenoaks as Australia, there is a farm called '*Sevenoaks*', named in Cedric's honour, by a boy he once supported financially.

A Survivor of the *Lusitania*

Hugh Martin Donald Gore Whitcombe, was born in 1894 in Suffolk, the son of John Walker Whitcombe and his wife, Katherine Louisa née Linnall. By 1901, the family were living in Sevenoaks. The 1911 census records Hugh as an engineer at a motor car works in Coventry. He left for the USA and then Cuba in February 1912, sailing on the *Lusitania* where his occupation was recorded as chauffeur.

Three years later in 1915, Hugh was once again aboard *Lusitania* sailing from Havana, Cuba and returning to England in order to enlist. According to his interview with the *Kent Messenger*, the passengers were having lunch in the dining saloon about four flights below deck when he heard a big bang '*and the plates and everything on the tables were upset, and fell into their laps*'. He stated that everyone knew at once what had happened but took things calmly, the males keeping their seats, until the ladies and children were got up to the boat deck. '*Some ladies fainted but the babies, not understanding what happened, remained happy*'.

Hugh then made his way to the boat deck and helped get women and children into the lifeboats. The ship had listed heavily to starboard the moment she was struck bringing that side high out of the water and the rescue rafts on the port side could not be used. According to Hugh's account, the sinking was so rapid that the other lifeboats were only just away

Sevenoaks Survivor Interviewed.

Mr. Hugh Donald Whitcombe, son of Mr. and Mrs. Whitcombe, of Dudbrook, Eardley Road, Sevenoaks, was a passenger on the ill-fated Cunarder, Lusitania. Just before the vessel sank he dived off and eventually was saved. He reached his home on Sunday.

Interviewed by a representative of the "Kent Messenger," Mr. Whitcombe said he was coming to this country from Havana, Cuba (where he had joined the Army Medical Service Corps), for the purpose of perfecting his training and bidding good-bye, prior to leaving for the Front. The passengers were having lunch

How the *Kent Messenger* reported Hugh's story

before the ship went down, while many boats *'were struck by the funnels and were taken down by the boat itself'*. Only 12 of the original 19 boats got away.

Hugh had stayed onboard with two of the ship's engineers and some of the stewards, waiting until the last minute, when they were nearly waist deep in water. Very shortly before the ship sank, they dived off and he became entangled with some of the wireless telegraph gear, which dragged him underwater. He managed to struggle free and swam for 15 minutes until he met a raft containing the two engineers he had been stood with and an elderly couple:

The water was full of struggling men and women. We managed to drag onto our raft a lady whose hand and leg had been badly crushed, and a little later a lady who was holding a dead child. We then manoeuvred our raft to an upturned boat and clambered on to it and remained drifting about until we were picked up by a destroyer, It was a horrible time – terrible! The elderly gentleman became exhausted and died before we were picked up, and we had to take the dead child from its mother, as the poor woman was growing frantic.

After three hours in the water, they were picked up by the first destroyer from Queenstown and taken to the town.

'It was', Hugh told the press, *'a terrible sight to see wives looking for their husbands, husbands for their wives and children for their parents'*.

Hugh had been travelling with five pounds worth of tobacco and cigarettes, sent by Cuban planters for the Indian soldiers – all of this and his own possessions were lost. Arriving safely in Sevenoaks, he said that despite some stiffness and bruises and a cut from a wire across the leg, he was little the worse for his experience.

The sinking of the *Lusitania* was a significant moment in the war. With 128 American lives lost, the ship's sinking sparked outrage in England and the USA and is generally credited as having played a key role in turning American public opinion against Germany.

Hugh went on to serve with the Army Service Corps and later with the Royal Flying Corps, being awarded the Belgian Croix de Guerre. Having survived the war and the sinking of the Lusitania, he died of sunstroke on 23rd July 1920, and was buried in the Mikra British Cemetery in Kalamria, Greece.

The Bassett Family at War

George Sidney Bassett (1892-1917) was the only member of the large and long-lived Bassett family to be killed during the war. He was born in Sevenoaks in 1879, was attached to 10th Battalion, Lancashire Fusiliers and had gone to supervise some wiring that his men were undertaking when he was hit in the face by a bullet from an enemy machine gun. He was carried to a first-aid post and died of his wounds. Second Lieutenant Edgar Hurst wrote to George's parents, Charles (1861-1935) and Adelaide (1860-1956):

> *I had learnt to like him very much in the few weeks I had known him. He was my favourite of the officers of our company and I have since heard the men say how they liked him. It is one great crying shame that such good lives should be wasted in such an awful war...*

George was not the only member of his family to play a role during the war, in fact, several of the men and women of the Bassett family served their country in different ways. His brother, Herbert William Bassett (1887-1950) fought with 6th (later 18th) London Rifles and was in France from March 1915.He wrote to the *Kent Messenger* from 'Somewhere in France' on 27th February 1916:

> *I am very thankful I am privileged to write this letter under the roof of a peasant's cottage in frozen Flanders, for outside it is decidedly like some old romance of Christmas-tide, and I must confess my thoughts during this week, have been of Sevenoaks, when tobogganing and skating have been in full swing in Knole Park. But matters have not been so pleasant for our men in the trenches, and during their tiring journeys in a blizzard to and from the firing line,. They struggle along ice covered roads, their heads bent to the storm, snow clinging to their greatcoats and stinging their faces like sharp crystals…*
>
> *   Great difficulties are experienced by the supply columns moving up from railheads to their various depots, with the whirling flakes blinding the drivers, horses slipping on the ice-bound roads, and wheels skidding from side to side, but the men are all very cheerful and light-hearted, in fact, they have revelled in the noise-less bursting of a snowball 'grenade' and many 'fights' have been witnessed on the white and desolate fields of Flanders, so please don't imagine the procession of troops along these roads was like the stragglers of Napoleon's Army in the great retreat from Moscow,. No, these men were going into the trenches, to play a more desperate game, and live bombs would be substituted for the harmless snowball.*

Gilbert Bassett in his
RFC uniform

George and Herbert's uncle, Gilbert Bassett (1879-1935), was with the Royal Flying Corps as Gunner/Observer G Bassett 60561, 62nd Squadron.

During the war he was apparently shot down behind

enemy lines and his belongings were returned to his mother as he was reported missing. He then turned up in a hospital in Folkestone but further details on this incident are scarce.

Gilbert recorded many of his experiences in his diary:

TRIP NO.2 – JUNE 11th

We started away from Lympne at 2.30 of the afternoon of June 11th and after an uneventful voyage of 35 minutes, with Lt Shaw as pilot, we landed at Marques and made a very good landing indeed. After stopping there a few minutes to get all particulars we took off again and headed south and finally landed at a place called Verton after a run of 25 minutes. He over judged the distance across the aerodrome and before he could turn the machine round he had run into a potato field and if the potatoes had been fit for digging the owners would have had them dug up gratis, but with our 700 horse power engines it got out alright. We were taken down to the mess to tea and a tender was ready for us afterwards to take us to Boulogne, where we arrived safely after having two burst tyres on the road. Stopped the night in Boulogne at 'Peters' and paid 3 francs for a bed and 1 franc 75c for breakfast then proceeded to the boat at 11.30 and after a very nice voyage arrived back in Blighty safe and sound after a very short journey of two days.

Gilbert Bassett – Front row 2nd from left 1917

TRIP NO.3 – JUNE 13th

When we arrived back from the previous trip we find there is another HP for us so on the 13th June we stand by that one and at 3.30 we make another move and after 40 minutes run we arrive in Marques. Again with Lt Shaw as pilot. It was too late then to catch the boat so stop in Marques the night and as usual sleep on the stage. Next morning we get a tender to take us to Bologne and the boat leaves at 12.15 and arrive back in Blighty all safe as per usual, but nothing doing in the way of excitement on these short trips worse luck and its getting monotonous.

Gilbert had been born in Seal and worked there as a builder before the war. Afterwards, he returned home to Seal where he ran the local garage, builders and coffin makers. He eventually moved to Hastings in the 1930s and died there aged 56.

Gilbert's niece and the sister of George Sidney and Herbert, Ada Margaret Bassett, known as Maggie, was born in 1897 and joined the Women's Royal Naval Service or WRENS at its formation in 1917 when she was only the fifth to enrol with the new service. Maggie became an official driver, working for Admiral Lord Jellicoe, who was then First Sea Lord. Later she served in the Second World War in the Auxiliary Transport Service and was a member of the First Aid Nursing Yeomanry, driving ambulances on the Home Front.

Two other brothers were also serving members of the forces. Charles Harold Bassett was an air mechanic in the Royal Flying Corps; Thomas Percy Bassett joined the Rifle Brigade in August 1917 having reached his 18th birthday. Of their brothers-in-law, Lieutenant Stanley Hocken was serving on a ship which the *Chronicle* noted *'had been launched from the Clyde shipyard, on which occasion Mrs Hocken (Edith nee Bassett) had the honour of performing the naming ceremony'*. Thomas Gibbs, husband of Helen Bassett, served with the Dorset Yeomanry.

The matriarch of the family, Ann Bassett née Parsons, the mother of George and Maggie's father, Charles, was born in 1835 and lived on until 1933. With youngest son Gilbert and grandchildren George, Herbert, Charles, Thomas and Maggie all serving, Ann became a tireless contributor to the war effort by knitting clothing for soldiers at the Front. She was thanked after the war as this photograph shows.

Ann Bassett, matriarch of the family,
was thanked for her contribution to the war effort

The Bassetts were the subject of an article in the *Sevenoaks Chronicle* entitled *'Patriotic Sevenoaks Family'* in June 1918. Their stories illustrate the range of ways that just one family from Sevenoaks contributed to the war effort.

Airmen of Sevenoaks

The Royal Flying Corps was the newest of the armed forces. Initially used only for reconnaissance to support bombardment of enemy positions by the artillery, the RFC's role grew rapidly and its technology developed throughout the war. Flying remained a dangerous occupation and many men were killed in accidents rather than in combat. Parachutes were not used primarily owing to their extra weight and size. There are five men who served with the Royal Flying Corps named on the Sevenoaks War Memorial: Bernard Vernon Gordon, George Walford, Nimrod King, Thomas Sillis and George Walford.

Just over a week before Bernard's death, his brother Cedric, who was himself serving with the RFC by this time wrote to him:

9th December 1916, letter to 2nd Lieut BV Gordon at the Aerodrome, Cramlington.

How are you getting on? I am glad you have got over your Preliminary part. I hope you still like flying. What sort of a pilot are you turning out to be? How long will it probably be before you get your wings? Life out here in the Winter is pretty dull. I have only been up twice in the last 3 weeks & there is nothing to do. They have just started quite a decent officers' club here. I am going there for dinner tonight. We have been having dreadfully dud weather here. Not much chance of it clearing up 'till about April. A Hun who was out on a night bombing raid lost his way & landed about 2 miles from here 3 nights ago. He only broke his prop. so he did pretty well. There was a great soccer match this afternoon. There is quite a lot of footer out here; I wish I could play & the fellows who can play don't want to! We have got a very good aerodrome here. The Hun prisoners have made a good job of it. There have been one or two very good concert

Bernard Vernon Gordon

parties down this way lately & there is to be a boxing show on this week. You ought to try boxing one day, it's quite good fun & very good exercise. Let me know if I can do anything for you. Who have you got as your Sqdn Commander & Flight Commanders? Nice people I hope. There are a lot of blighters in the Corps.

Well, very best of luck. Cheerho.

Bernard was killed, aged 18, in an aircraft crash near Newcastle on 14th December 1916, his 13th Solo sortie.

The exploits of other local RFC men were often reported in the *Sevenoaks Chronicle*.

Ernest Horncastle was one such man. A son of Walter Horncastle, a tailor based in the High Street (a family business which still operates today), Ernest was born in Sevenoaks in 1890. Aged 23 and at 6'1 and in good health, he enlisted in August 1914 and soon received a temporary commission with the Royal Field Artillery, arriving in France that December. After a few months he was attached to the Royal Flying Corps Balloon Section. In August 1917 the *Sevenoaks Chronicle* reported that Ernest:

...has seen some very stiff work and had some thrilling experiences.

By 1917, Ernest was suffering from shell shock and fever and spent a period of five weeks on leave at home. A Medical Board report concluded that his illness was due to active service and that he *'is very neurotic and complaining of subjective symptoms'.*

Ernest recovered well enough to return to service and continued until early 1918 when he was diagnosed with bronchitis and neurasthenia (nervous exhaustion) and was sent to hospital before returning home on leave to England. A Medical Board held in that March noted that his bronchitis had cleared but that he still suffered from muscular pains and other symptoms.

The medical officer's opinion was that:

He has done a good deal of active service. It is highly probable that his nerve for flying is failing or has done so. He is otherwise perfectly well.

In fact, by this time, Ernest had clocked up over 150 hours flying. The board concluded that Ernest should return to some duty, in order for his mind to be distracted from himself:

(he) leads an ordinary life of pleasure and enjoyment and takes plenty of exercise. He has greatly improved in every way since admission.

Ernest survived the war and lived until 1964.

Another Ernest, a brother of soldier Leonard Brooker who is remembered on the town War Memorial, initially served with the Royal Engineers. The *Sevenoaks Chronicle* reported in September 1917 that Ernest:

is engaged in wireless telegraphy work. He has been in France eighteen months and finds his work pleasurable.

Ernest Brooker

A chemist in civilian life, Ernest joined the RFC and survived the war but was killed in a motor accident in 1929.

Horace Owen was born in 1890, the son of local councillor, Richard, and his wife, Laura. Initially he joined the Royal Naval Volunteer Reserve. Horace later transferred to the Flying Corps, where he served as a temporary lieutenant.

The *Chronicle* reported in early 1917 that Horace had only recently left Sevenoaks to commence his duties in France as a member of the RFC but went missing after his first flight. After weeks of uncertainty, a letter from Horace arrived home informing his parents that he had been shot down while flying and was now a prisoner of war. Horace had been captured on 28th March 1917 and was repatriated on 14th January 1919. He lived on until 1969.

Frederick Herbert St Clair Sargant (1897–1968) was another young Sevenoaks airman. The *Chronicle* recounted some of his exploits in an article entitled *Sevenoaks Aviator's Exciting Experience in 1916*:

> *Owing to engine trouble I got separated from the others on a bombing raid and was attacked by five Huns. My engine, petrol tank, and rudder controls were shot through and I started coming down in a spinning nose-dive from 8,000 feet. The Huns followed me down, but we managed to land the 'bus' in a shell hole just behind our lines. We both ran as hard as we could, as they started shelling the wrecked machine almost at once. I was hit by a machine gun bullet from one of the Huns aeroplanes. My observer was unhurt.*

Howard Reeder Daws, was just 17 when he joined the Royal Flying Corps in October 1915. Daws was the son of William and his wife, Sarah, who ran a confectionary shop and lived at Bank Street, Sevenoaks. He was posted to No. 5 Squadron and based at St Omer. He was at Ypres from 1915 until he was hospitalised in the summer of 1916. After recovering and taking courses in observing and gunnery, he returned to active service, based at Lympne. In

Howard Reeder Daws

May 1917 he recorded that he *'flew the channel for the first time in Bristol Fighter A/7114. Pilot Lt Barker, Crashed at St Omer'*. The injuries later caused him to lose his leg, although they were not apparent at the time.

After the war, Daws settled in Green Street Green, where he ran a shop. He died in 1969.

Ivan Hart-Davies (1878-1917), had been a schoolmaster at the New Beacon School in Sevenoaks and counted Siegfried Sassoon amongst his pupils. Himself the son of a vicar, he also

Ivan Hart-Davies

taught the sons of the Rector of St Nicholas and the Rev. Thompson of St Mary, Kippington. Hart-Davies had left the school and obtained a commission in the RFC by the time of his death, which was reported in *The Times*:

> *Lieutenant Ivan Beauclerk Hart-Davies, RFC, who was killed in an aeroplane accident in England was the son of the late Rev John Hart-Davies of Southam Rectory, Warwickshire and was 39 years of age. He was educated at a school at Maidenhead and at King's School, Canterbury, and began life as a schoolmaster at New Beacon, Sevenoaks. Afterwards, however, he worked up a wide life insurance and motor insurance business in the Midlands. He held the 'end-to-end' 'record' for motor cycles and light cars, and in 1913, with three other motorcyclists, won the Murren Cup, though none of the four had done any bobsleighing before. He took to flying before the war as an amateur, but last year he obtained a commission in the RFC and was on the eve of going to the Front. A brother officer writes 'A gallant fellow who we all liked immensely, and are deeply grieved that he should have been fatally injured when he so much wished to go to France, where doubtless he would have won honours'.*

Harry Watson Durtnell

Harry Watson Durtnell was a scion of the Durtnell family of Brasted, builders since the reign of Elizabeth I. Harry was a cousin of Richard Neville Durtnell who was killed in action in 1917. Initially serving with the Welch regiment, Harry later transferred to serve with the RFC. He survived the war, living until 1971.

Many other local men served with the RFC at all levels in the new service. John Potter had worked with his father for five years in the Blacksmiths Forge at Knole and had joined the army in November 1916 aged 19. Putting his training to good use, the *Sevenoaks Chronicle* reported that he had been selected for *'flying machines repair work'* and was employed in the Royal Naval Flying Corps workshops.

Herbert Terry DCM

Herbert Terry was born in Sevenoaks in 1887 to Arthur Jasper Terry (1861–1916) and his wife, Margaret Eliza née Spavins (1857–1946). The 1901 census shows the family living on Hartslands Road, with Arthur working as a gardener and 13 year old Herbert described as a 'cyclists boy', possibly for the Post Office.

Herbert with wife, Mary, and eldest son
Arthur, who was also given the name of Mons

Herbert was 27 and working as a gardener when he enlisted shortly after the war began at Maidstone Barracks on 7th September 1914. His service papers show that he was 5ft 6½ with a dark complexion, blue eyes and black hair. He initially joined the 7th Battalion, Royal West Kent Regiment, was later transferred to 9th Battalion in July 1915 and then in August of that year to the 8th. Herbert had married Mary Maria Mercer (1894–1966) in early 1914 and his first son, Arthur Bertram Mons Terry, was born later that year, to be followed by five other children. Children born during the war were often given the names of particular battles, such as Mons or Verdun, as one of their names.

According to his service papers, Herbert did not leave for the Front until 1st October

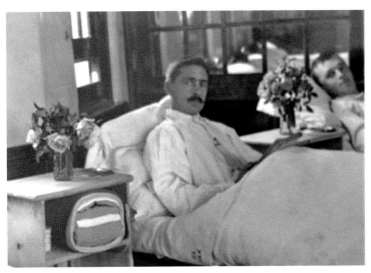

Herbert in hospital in 1917

1915. He had an unblemished record (apart from once slightly overstaying his leave which led to his forfeiting one day's pay) and he was promoted to lance corporal, then acting corporal, and finally to corporal in the autumn of 1916.He was promoted to sergeant the following year and was awarded the Distinguished Conduct Medal in early 1918. According to the citation in the *London Gazette* of 17th April 1918 he received the medal '*For conspicuous gallantry and devotion to duty. He was one of a party which entered the enemy's trenches and captured two prisoners. He has continually done excellent patrol work and has set a splendid example of courage and good leadership during a long period*'.

Some months before this on 24th July 1917, Herbert sustained a shell wound to his left leg, which was subsequently amputated. He spent some time in a hospital in St Albans recovering from his operation and was honourably discharged in September 1918.

At the time the *Chronicle* noted that:

Mrs Terry of Bushes Road (now Prospect Road) received the news that her husband, Sergeant Herbert Terry, had his left leg blown off in the recent fighting.

According to Barry Hillier, his grandfather, William Watson Hillier, served with Bert Terry in the 8th Battalion and was with him when he was injured. William lived at Kemsing and before the war was a railway signalman. According to William, he and Bert were sent to take a message back to HQ. On the way Bert was hit. William tended to his wound, applied a tourniquet and left him whilst he delivered the message. He returned soon after and took him to a first aid post. William was later wounded at Ypres and returned to the UK. Having saved Bert's life, the pair became friends and would occasionally drink together in civilian life.

After the war, Herbert worked at the Sevenoaks Telephone Exchange as male supervising telephonist, for many years being in charge of the night staff. He retired after 30 years' service, with another profile in the *Sevenoaks Chronicle* and recalled how the night staff had once consisted of himself and one assistant, having since grown to more than 20. He also recalled hectic nights during the Second World War *'with 80 copies of the war communique to write out in between the passing of air-raid warning messages to exchanges and civil defence units throughout the area'.*

Herbert enjoyed a long retirement and died in 1976 aged 89. He is buried in Greatness Cemetery.

A Postcard Home

An embroidered silk postcard from the First World War, in good condition and with the soldier's name and number written clearly, as well as the name of the recipient, was a clue to the story of one interesting local family.

Silk postcards, like this one sent by Charlie Draper, were an important form of communication for those on the Western Front

It was sent by Sapper 24682 C Draper of WR 334 Road Construction Company of the Royal Engineers.

This was Charlie Draper of Sevenoaks. Charlie's records show that he was 29 and working as an engine driver when he was called up in February 1917. On enlistment he had expressed a desire to join the Royal Engineers Road Construction Company.

According to his records, Charlie was living at 3, Morants Cottages, Cramptons Road, Sevenoaks with his wife, Elsie Nellie Draper née Porter, (whom he had married on Boxing Day 1911 in Kippington, Sevenoaks) and his daughter, Elsie Doris, born 1912.

It seems likely that Charlie was employed by the Kent County Council as a letter from the County Surveyor is preserved in his file, which shows that the Council had supported his request to work for the road units in France.

Charlie was sent overseas on 1st March 1917 when he embarked at Southampton bound for Le Havre. In October 1917 he passed a test and was regraded to the skilled rate of engineer pay. The Road Construction Companies performed vital work throughout the war and Charlie's peacetime skills were no doubt invaluable. Charlie's army service continued until January 1920. He served with 334 Road Construction Company until 24th May 1919, and was then transferred via the base depot to the 5th Transportation Stores Company.

Charlie, as he was christened, was one of seven children born to Charles Draper and his wife, Bertha née Welfare. Charles Draper senior was well known locally as a cricketer and the landlord of The Halfway House, a pub still open, not far from Sevenoaks train station on the way to Riverhead.

Through his mother, Bertha, granddaughter of John Wells, Charlie was a second cousin once removed of the writer H. G. Wells who wrote the first English science fiction novel, *The Time Machine*, whilst lodging at 23, Eardley Road, Sevenoaks.

Charles Draper senior was born in Penshurst in 1860 and had been landlord of the Halfway House for 15 years when he died on 14th May 1903 at Guy's Hospital in London. For a pub landlord, Charles received a fulsome obituary in the *Sevenoaks Chronicle*, a testament perhaps not only to his prowess as a cricketer but also to his personality. He appears to have been much mourned.

The *Sevenoaks Chronicle* reported that:

By his death Sevenoaks loses one of its most celebrated cricketers. From an early age he was more than ordinarily proficient both with the bat and ball and all through his life, up to the last season or so, he has been a most consistent and successful player. For many years he was groundsman to the Vine and it was largely owing to his exertions that the old Vine club was enabled for so many years to maintain its reputation.

Cricket clearly ran in the family as Charles's father, William (1823-1901), had been a cricket ball maker, while his brother, William (1848-1919) had played first class cricket for Kent from 1874-1880. Another brother, Henry (1847-1896), was a test match umpire. William's son, Herbert, also served during the war with the Royal Engineers only to die during the Spanish Flu pandemic in November 1919.

Charles's obituary noted that he left a widow and seven children, the eldest being 17.

The *Chronicle* later recorded that the pub licence had been transferred to Bertha but by 1911 she was living at 14, Holyoake Terrace with Charlie, aged 23 and recorded as a traction engine driver, and five of her other children, including Frank, aged 15, a butcher's assistant. A daughter, Bertha, was residing at 118 High Street at Whyntie & Co.

Charlie survived the war, leaving the army in 1920 and living until 1959 when it appears that he died, aged 71, in the St Albans area.

Charlie's younger brother, Frank Draper, enlisted at Tonbridge in September 1914 shortly after the outbreak of war. He was posted abroad in June 1915. By 1916 he had been promoted to Corporal, serving with 6th Battalion of the Royal West Kent Regiment. Unlike his brother, Frank did not survive the war. He was killed in action in May 1917; the date of his death assumed to be 3rd. Frank is remembered both on the Arras Memorial and on the Sevenoaks War Memorial.

What of the of recipient of the postcard, Miss West, who was perhaps living or visiting at Charlie's home at Morants Cottages when the postcard was sent? There is no way of identifying her with any degree of certainty. None of Charlie's sisters appears to have married a Mr West. The one family with that surname who lived nearby to the Draper family, on Moor Road, did have one daughter of the right age in the 1911 census but she had died by the likely posting of the card in early 1917.

∼

Part Four

CONSCRIPTION & TRIBUNALS

Stories from the Tribunal

Despite the flow of volunteers into the ranks of Kitchener's New Army, and other initiatives such as the Derby Scheme, it became apparent that conscription would have to be introduced to supply the men the army required. The Military Service Act introduced conscription in January 1916, meaning that single men between the ages of 18 and 41 became eligible for military service. A second Act was introduced that May. This extended conscription to married men. A network of Military Service Tribunals was then established to hear the cases of men who wished to be exempted from being called up. Although approximately 2000 tribunals operated across the country, few records survive, which is why the records of proceedings as reported in local papers are invaluable. Some men appealing were conscientious objectors, while others were seeking exemptions because they worked on the land, cared for family members or worked in reserved occupations.

Members of the tribunal were invariably drawn from the ranks of the middle and upper classes who would hear each case before deciding on its merits. The person appealing could be represented by a solicitor or even a relative or employer and both the applicant and military representative had the right of appeal to a further tribunal. The *Kent Messenger* reported that nearly 20 cases from the Sevenoaks division came before the West Kent Appeal Tribunal in Maidstone in November 1916. These cases were appeals against prior decisions at a local tribunal.

The *Messenger* noted that the panel included Earl Amherst and Sir Mark Collet (of the St Clere estate at Heverham, Kemsing village, near Sevenoaks), and detailed a number of the cases concerning residents from Sevenoaks from all walks of life. From orchid growers and veterans of the Boer War, to one man who was subsequently killed in action and remembered on the Sevenoaks War Memorial, the *Messenger* reported their cases, some of which caused laughter at the time:

Charles Digby Robertson, 40, of the Rose and Crown Hotel, who was represented by

FRIDAY, NOVEMBER 24, 1916.

West Kent Appeal Tribunal.

Interesting Cases from the Sevenoaks Division.

Nearly twenty cases from the Sevenoaks Division came before the West Kent Appeal Tribunal at the Sessions House, Maidstone, on Thursday, when the members present were: Mr. Roland Allen (chairman), Earl Amherst, Sir J. Brombead Matthews, Messrs. J. Barker, C. Tuff and A. W. Tapp, with Mr. W. B. Prosser (clerk), Sir Mark Collet (agricultural representative), and Mr. Vaughan Gower (military representative).

Frank Arthur Smith, 36, motor and general smith, Brasted, explained that he was doing work of national importance in making aeroplane parts, and in doing other Government work. He was classified C3.

The Tribunal gave him three months' exemption, conditional on his continuing to do similar work as that upon which he is now engaged.

Charles Digby Robertson, 40, of the Rose and Crown Hotel, Sevenoaks, was represented by Mr. Brennan, who asked for time in which the wife could be educated in conducting the business. Appellant, who quite recognised he would have to join the army, had only been at the hotel about a year and previously he kept a public-house at Wrotham.

Thinking the wife must have already acquired some experience, the appeal was dismissed, but directions given that Mr. Robertson should not be called up before December 15th.

How the *Kent Messenger* reported on the Tribunal

Mr Brennan asked for time during which his wife could be educated in conducting the business. Appellant, who quite recognised that he would have to join the army, had only been at the hotel about a year and previously he kept a public house at Wrotham.

Thinking the wife must already have acquired some experience, the appeal was dismissed, but directions given that Mr Robertson should not be called up before December 15th.

The tribunal dismissed the appeal of Caleb Newman, 39, of the Greyhound Hotel, Sevenoaks, but in order that he could arrange his affairs, they directed that he should not be called up for a month. Mr H J Brader, who represented the appellant, elicited that he was classified B1, that he served in the South African War, receiving the medal and five clasps, and afterwards remained in the South Africa Mounted Police for three years.

The case of John William Terry, 18, working for his father, a Sevenoaks farrier, was dismissed, although the local tribunal had described it as 'a hard case'. It was stated that eight blacksmiths had left Sevenoaks for the army and munition work, and that Mr Terry's other son, having joined the colours he took this lad from the butchering trade to assist him in the farrier's shop.

Robert James Buckle, single, orchid grower for Mr Phillips, Sevenoaks, was represented by Mr Knight, who called in question his ability to serve in C1, to which class he had been allocated. He produced a certificate from a local doctor, showing that for 16 years he had suffered from varicose veins, which were very bad now. The panel declined an invitation to view the appellants' legs for themselves and dismissed the appeal, stating that while it was true C1 men were being called up, he would undergo another medical examination on joining the colours.

Mr M Blake sought exemption for his cowman, Albert Elvy, 32, single, Dunton Green, and said if the man left he should be compelled to reduce his herd. He stated, in answer to questions, that he did not think it right to ask ladies to do continuous milking, and to laughter said that one he did employ was kicked by a cow, and would not come again!

Bert Wallis was appealed for by his father, a builder in Sevenoaks. The local tribunal had suggested that Mr Wallis snr with his clerk could manage the business. This Mr Wallis denied, saying it was quite impossible for the clerk to do the work of his son, which included the preparing of estimates, and getting out quantities etc. Already eight of his employees had joined the army. This case also saw an exchange which provoked some laughter:

Sir John Matthews: *How many builders are there in Sevenoaks?*

Mr Wallis: *Oh! The place is eaten up with them*

Sir John: *Why don't the builders of Sevenoaks cooperate then?*

Mr Wallis: *We are too much at variance for that!*

Percy John French, single, a hairdresser, asked for a few months' respite so that in the meantime he could give further training to his brother, who could then carry on the business while he was away. It transpired that his brother was originally apprenticed to the business, and had joined the army, but was discharged ten months ago and had since been assisting in the work of the barber's shop. The tribunal declined to interfere with the decision of the local tribunal beyond directing that appellant should not be called up for a fortnight. Mr House, defending the case stated that he understood that the commanding officer of the Essex Yeomanry, who was stationed near Sevenoaks, was willing to take appellant as regimental barber, which would allow him the opportunity of keeping eye on his own business. The Chairman said that they could not do anything in that direction.

Ernest George Palmer, 32, caterer, of 98, High Street, Sevenoaks, caused some amusement by the way he referred to his wife. Asked if he was married he replied in the affirmative and then enquiry was made as to his children, he said that he had none, adding *'I have a large wife and a small family!'*

The Chairman: *I thought that you said you had no children*

Mr Palmer: *No, I have not.*

Palmer went on to state that although he was originally rejected, he had now been passed for general service, notwithstanding the fact that he was deaf in one ear.

The chairman: *Could not your wife manage this catering business?*

Palmer said that he did not think so, as a man was required, seeing there were many soldiers about and they had already had trouble with them. He added, to laughter:

You see my wife cannot get about as quick as the soldiers!

The tribunal dismissed his appeal but gave instructions that he should not be called up before December 31st.

The *Messenger* also reported some cases heard in the Sevenoaks Urban Tribunal.

> *W A Taylor, of Varennes Lodge, South Park, organist at St Luke's, and music teacher at the Beacon Schools, said he was 41 years of age on June 24th, the day appointed by the military authorities in fixing the age limit. Had he been born an hour earlier he would have been exempt (laughter). The application was refused on the understanding that Mr Johnson would write to the recruiting officer asking him not to call upon Mr Taylor before the end of the school term.*
>
> *Mr De Barri Crawshay, of Rosefield, Sevenoaks, applied for his son, Lionel Crawshay and said that he (the father) was appointed transport officer to the VAD hospitals in 1915, when there were eight hospitals with 244 beds. The number had now increased to ten hospitals and 400 beds. The son was his chief assistant. He also appealed on the grounds of his son's ill health, but it was stated that he had been passed for general service. One month was allowed but the Tribunal, while appreciating the service thus rendered, were of the opinion that an older man could do the work.*

Lionel Crawshay subsequently enlisted in Maidstone on 28th December 1916, first with the Reserve Battalion of the 2nd Life Guards at Windsor, later transferring to 2/4th Battalion, The Queen's (Royal West Surrey) Regiment. Crawshay was later one of 50 men selected to be sent to Egypt, with a view to receiving his commission. He was sent initially to France, spending a few days in a rest camp before embarking for Egypt on board the hired transport ship the *SS Transylvania*. The *Transylvania* was sunk by a torpedo on 4th May. Lionel, along with 400 others, drowned. His body was recovered and he was buried in the Savona Town Cemetery, which contains the graves of many of those who perished with him.

The work of the tribunals continued throughout the war. In March 1918, it heard the case of Albert Iddenden, 32, head waiter at the Royal Crown Hotel. Iddenden had been classified as B1 and stated that he had twice attempted to join the Hussars, only to be rejected as medically unfit each time. He had eight children under ten and the tribunal committee considered that the separation allowance due to his wife would be a total of 41 shillings. Iddenden stated that his father had been a sergeant major in the 14th Hussars and seven of his brothers had served in the South African War. This remarkable fact had come to the attention of Queen Victoria herself, who commanded her then private secretary, Frederick Ponsonby, to write to Iddenden's mother (who had had 17 pregnancies, 10 of whom survived), enclosing a £5 note. Albert Iddenden's case was adjourned to allow him to find work of national importance.

Conscientious Objectors

After the introduction of the Military Service Act in 1916, many local men appeared before the local Military Tribunal to seek an exemption from service on religious grounds.

As conscientious objectors they stated that they could not take another man's life. The Act allowed for objectors to be absolutely exempted, to perform alternative civilian service, or to serve as a non-combatant according to the decision of the tribunal.

Around 16,000 men were recorded as conscientious objectors nationally: 9000 objectors accepted alternative service and were often sent to do work of national importance, such as farming. 3,300 were sent to the newly formed Non Combatant Corps. Many others were imprisoned at least once. Even so, cases relating to conscientious objectors formed a small percentage of the Military Service Tribunals' work.

As most of the files for conscientious objectors were destroyed in the 1920's, newspaper reports are an important source of information.

In March 1916, Charles Edward Farrant, 26, of 42, Cobden Road, was a cowman employed by Robert Mond at Combe Bank, and applied for absolute exemption on religious grounds. His case was supported by his employer, who stated that he was looking after pure bred stock. He asserted that his religious views meant that on no account could he fight. His application was refused and he was recommended for non-combatant service.

Harold John Mann was a 22 year old schoolmaster of '*Heatherleigh*', Dartford Road, employed at the New Beacon School. Mann stated that the religious views he had been brought up with prevented him from taking life in any circumstances. He also had to support his mother. In his case a temporary exemption was granted for three months.

Leslie Frank Hoad was living at 2 Gilehurst Villas, Argyle Road and had been employed as a draper's assistant, when he appeared before the Sevenoaks Tribunal in September 1916. The fact of his conscientious objection was accepted without argument and Hoad stated that he had given up his job to work in agriculture near Swanley to demonstrate that he was willing to do something of which the country had need.

The committee refused to grant an exemption. His case came before the West Kent Tribunal in January 1917. This tribunal granted him an exemption for three months, conditional upon him remaining in employment on the land. Leslie was working as a motor tractor driver when next reported as having been granted a further four month extension when he appeared before the county Tribunal again in July 1917.

Alfred Mannington Sayers appeared before the tribunal in June 1916 and pleaded guilty to a charge of not reporting himself for military service. Detective Coley gave evidence against Sayers, stating that he declined to go because he was a conscientious objector. The defendant's father agreed that there was no doubt that his son was an absentee but argued that it was well understood that '*the tribunals had not administered the Act*'. The Chair denied this and highlighted the responsibility of the court to carry out the law; the defendant had been ordered to do something by a competent authority and had not done so. He went on to remark that:

> *defendant might be a perfectly amiable young man and did not want to hurt anyone at all, not even his country's enemies. The bench would accept that for him.*

The court then imposed a fine of 40 shillings and the defendant was handed over to a military escort.

De Barry Cox, aged 22, of 4, Barrack Corner, was another man arrested by Detective Coley for not reporting for military service on the grounds of conscientious objection. He was fined 50 shillings, which was to be deducted from his military pay, and handed over to the authorities.

Jack Harbour of Greatness Terrace who worked as a railway porter at Bat and Ball railway station was similarly charged. Harbour appealed on the grounds of his conscientious objection to fighting.

His case was dismissed after cross-examination. Judge Parry presiding asked:

What are you doing now?

Harbour: *I am a railway porter*

Judge: *The railways belong to the State, and are therefore a military organisation. A good many troops go through your station, so you help them in that way?*

Harbour: *That is my daily work.*

Records for both Cox and Harbour survive, showing that each served subsequently served in the war with the Non Combatant Corps.

Herbert Sears was another conscientious objector who served with the Non Combatant Corps. Sears had worked for the Rector of Sevenoaks, Reverend John Rooker, managing the Rectory farm. He died in October 1918 of pneumonia and is buried in the churchyard at St Nicholas, together with his wife who died only days after him.

Harry Raven, 33, of '*Sunnyside*', Clarendon Road, was the manager of a shirt making and hosiery business in Piccadilly. Raven claimed to be:

A true and consistent follower of the Lord Jesus Christ, whose commands he must obey. Thou shalt love thy God and thy neighbour as thy self

Raven was willing to do farm work, though he had no experience of it. The tribunal refused his case and recommended him for non-combatant service.

At the same hearing, James Samuel Bolton, a married signwriter of Bradbourne Villas, Bradbourne Road stated *'I hold it wrong to terminate human life unnaturally'.*

Thousands, he added, were suffering innocently owing to the use of arms, which secured the victory to the stronger side, whether it was in the right or wrong. Bolton said that he was not a member of any religious body and pleaded that he was only able to keep himself, his wife, and family without being a burden to the community, and without being able to take part in philanthropic work. He remarked that he was not averse to agricultural, railway or police work. The tribunal refused the case and Bolton declared that he would exercise his right to appeal.

George Mullen appeared before the tribunal in June 1918. Mullen was the manager of a grocery business in St John's for his employer, Mr Frank Rowley. Aged 44, he had been classified as grade 2 and his appeal had been supported by the local Food Control Committee (by casting vote of the Chairman). A solicitor for Mr Rowley stated that he had had bad health for two years and had 700 registered customers for sugar. Mr Mullen managed the business and been with him for 22 years. There were two other shops and the other manager was not fully qualified. It was revealed that Mullen was a member of the International Bible Students' Association and conducted meetings at Tunbridge Wells. Mullen was questioned on the information that he had a son of 18 serving in the navy, replying that he allowed his son to hold his own opinions.

Rowley's solicitor argued that if Mullen were taken, the business would have to close down as he was not fit enough to run it on his own and he could get no one else capable to run it for him. The tribunal dismissed the appeal but gave 56 days before call up in view of Mr Rowley's condition.

Many conscientious objectors worked on the farms in and around Sevenoaks. Some of these men were local but others were from further afield. Thirty-six year old Walter Flexman had been a manager and buyer in the books and stationary department at Hamleys store in London. Flexman had lived on Brondesbury Road, North London, but in 1916 was resident at 11, Bethel Road and working for Mr Wood of Greatness Farm.

Walter Flexman had been granted a conditional exemption from combat service only in August 1916 and was offered work on the farm from the September, at a rate of 3 shillings a day. In that December he was required to apply for a renewal of his exemption, which was supported by his employer on the farm, Mr Wood, who stated that after three months, Flexman was a real help; to lose him would be to lose valuable experience and require time in training new workers.

Walter Flexman was granted a renewal. At around the same time, Mr Wood appeared before the local tribunal in the case of a Mr Cheeseman, a worker on the farm. Cheeseman was described as a skilled farm labourer. Mr Wood stated that there were six conscientious objectors on the farm but they were not skilled farm hands and had taken the place of other men who had gone to fight.

A committee member asked how the men worked, to which Mr Wood's reply was laughter. Mr Cheeseman was given a conditional exemption.

On the limited evidence available, the Sevenoaks Tribunal appears to have conducted its hearings in a business-like way. Few men who appeared before it as conscientious objectors were granted complete exemptions. More often cases were dismissed and the applicant recommended for non-combatant service.

Public opinion generally viewed conscientious objectors with suspicion and disdain. The *Sevenoaks Chronicle* did occasionally carry criticism of conscientious objectors, from printing popular jokes to reporting the speech of the Earl of Denbigh when he visited Sevenoaks in January 1918. According to the Earl:

> *We should spare no effort to make the women understand the things the Germans did. Let the women of Kent think about it, because probably they might be the first to feel it. If the British women knew and realised one quarter of the German ideas; they would see to it that no conscientious objector would dare to show his contemptible face in the public street.*

The paper also printed criticism of objectors from serving soldiers. Rifleman H Woodfine from Hither Green, wrote a letter from Salonika in June 1916, which was printed in the

Chronicle (the writer's link to Sevenoaks is not noted). Woodfine wrote:

> *The boys are making huge fun of the conscientious objector. In the times of Nelson and Wellington, such people would be shot. They ought to go and see places like Mons, Ypres, Louvain, Rheims, and Alsace. I think this would alter their attitude.*

After the Armistice, a concerned parent wrote to the paper, indignant at the thought that the rights of conscientious objectors would be put before those who had served.

> *Dear Sir*
>
> *I saw in your last issue an appeal from one of the Territorials in India. I myself have a son serving there, who has been away for the past four years and a half, and who is anxious to return. The idea of releasing conscientious objectors before the man who has done his duty! I hope this will meet the eyes of those who shouted for the men to join! Are they still shouting to get them released?*
>
> *Yours faithfully,*
>
> *A DISGUSTED PARENT*

Conscientious Objectors were still viewed with suspicion after the war and were not allowed to vote between 1918 and 1923. However, many of the objectors from Sevenoaks appear to have carried on living and working in the community after the war. George Mullen took over his former employer's shop when Frank Rowley died in 1922. During the Second World War, Alfred Sayers published a collection of poetry – *'Poems of 20 Years'* that the *Chronicle* featured prominently, which suggests that by then he viewed as a respected member of the local community.

My Father was a Conscientious Objector

Mollie Wren was born Ivy Florence Tester in 1912 in Sevenoaks to George Tester (1883-1962) and Emma née Banfield (1881-1960). Known as Mollie, she married Philip Wren and later in life moved to Somerset. In the early 1990's, Mollie, along with several other elderly women living in the Winsham area, talked about her childhood memories in an initiative run by the South Somerset Reminiscence Project, the results of which were published, with several of Mollie's family photos included. Mollie died in 1996 and bequeathed her father's memoirs, photographs and other items to her extended family. Her memories are clear and evocative of the challenges her family faced as a result of her father's stance, as they were abused, ignored and faced financial hardship.

The 1911 census shows Mollie's parents, George and Emma, living at 13, St Botolph's Road with their son, George Albert (1906-1994), with George senior recorded as a builder. The family were active members of the Vine Baptist Church. By 1916 the family had moved to Cedar Villa, Cedar Terrace and, that June, George was mentioned in the *Sevenoaks Chronicle* in its report on the proceedings of the local Military Tribunal. In its 23rd June edition, the paper noted that George:

George Tester and Emma Banfield on their wedding day

wanted to save life rather than take it, but did not object to non-combatant service, to which he was referred.

George's military records show that he was 33½, five feet tall, and working as a painter when he subsequently enrolled with the Non Combatant Corps in July 1916. That December,

The family at Seaford Cliffs

George was working at Newhaven when he was charged with disobeying a lawful command given to him by an officer while on active service. He was tried by court martial and sentenced to be detained at Wormwood Scrubs.

Mollie recalled these events:

Father said no, he wasn't going to fight. He just simply believed Thou Shalt Not Kill. He was sent with a lot of others to Seaford Cliffs to load food ships for the troops. He continued with that until they wanted him to load firearms. They all refused. So then he was sent to Lewes gaol and court-martialled. He was tried by Lord Salisbury, who was sympathetic to conscientious objectors. Even so, he sent my father to Wandsworth prison for a year in solitary confinement, and then to Dartmoor Prison for two years and seven months.

George (third right) in the workshop at Wormwood Scrubs

As a family, we were ostracised. I remember walking hand in hand with mother along St John's Road. Two men, up ladders, shouted something abusive at my mother. She gripped my hand tightly and hurried me away. Father had said mother must continue to go to the Baptist church, although no-one spoke to her. I remember walking up the aisle to our pew, which was halfway up the church. My mother held my hand tightly.

A couple of teachers at Sevenoaks Council School were horrible to me because my dad had been a conscientious objector. They felt very strongly.

As my father was a conscientious objector, my mother had no government pay, and in the end she was virtually penniless. One night she knelt at the armchair by the cold grate in the kitchen, and prayed to God to help her. Even as she prayed the front door rattled, and she heard something put through the letterbox. She went through the passage and there was an envelope on the mat. No letter in it, but a five pound note, which in those days was a great deal of money. Mother never forgot this, and she always used to quote me afterwards: 'The barrel of meal shall not waste, neither shall the cruse of oil fail' (1 Kings 17:14). *And it never did. Finally, kind people came to their senses and brought Mother sewing. She was extremely able. People would bring their sewing on the quiet to start with, but at least it came.*

Robert Mond of Combe Bank, Sundridge, gave Home Farm over as a convalescent home for wounded officers and their batmen. Mother became the sewing woman here. Her eldest sister, Fanny, became cook-housekeeper, and my uncle became head cowman.

There was no shortage of food there, despite the war. My aunt was a typical cook of that generation: a large lady in a blue-print dress and snow-white apron, with her lovely hair brushed back. I can see her now, standing at the kitchen table with enormous tin plates covered in pastry, and a gallipot of jam clasped to her bosom, ladling jam onto these plates. Then they were cut in six for the wounded soldiers. They loved her pastry.

Not only was I spoiled by my aunt, but by the soldiers, I walked out with them in the country lanes and into Sundridge village, where they bought me sweets. A lot of them were married and had children of their own.

There was a great bronze gong hanging on a stand and a stick with a leather ball at the top, I loved sloshing this gong. The soldiers tried to teach me how to work up a real crescendo, but I was too little. I just loved banging it! On Sundays we went to Chevening church in a horse brake, which had seats on either side. There was I, in the middle of all these soldiers, going off to church!

There was one ward for the batmen, and the officers were in another. I remember the long rows of beds and red blankets. One particular officer was very fond of me, and when he was he dying asked to see me. Mother carried me upstairs and told me to be good. We went in with the Matron. I remember being sat on the bed. He held my hand, and his hand was very hot. I remember that clearly but no more.

In 1916, my mother took in a lodger, a Miss Bunting. This lady was a brilliant dressmaker. She'd been very adventurous and gone off to Russia and become one of the

Mollie with an officer at Combe Bank

Tsarina's court dressmakers. When the Revolution was boiling up, she fled home quickly. One night she tapped at the bedroom door and said, 'Mrs Tester, you must come quickly! You must see this!'. *My mother picked me up out of the cot, wrapped a shawl round me and carried me into her bedroom, which had a wonderful view over the North Downs. And there was this airship going along, a German airship. It had caught fire: it was blazing as it went along. I remember my mother murmuring over my head,* 'Poor souls, poor souls!'.

Father wasn't released from Dartmoor until 1919. I was seven. Mother couldn't go to the station to meet him after that separation, so my brother and I went. I remember running round the garden picking a bunch of flowers. It was perfectly ridiculous: I was going to meet this unknown 'Dad'. I remember getting to the station, and a cloud of steam; and out of it came this man whom my brother rushed to, because he remembered him. Then I remember being crushed, flowers and all, against this man. When we got to the garden gate, Mother, who had been standing watching in the sitting-room window, came to the front door. Father went in, and I was going to prance in after, but my brother hung on to the back of my frock and took me round the garden. He was more sensitive that for just a little while they wanted to be alone.

George senior, George and Mollie after the war

George Tester lived on until 1962, surviving his wife, Emma, by two years. His mother, Martha Tester née Letchford (1845-1946) lived to see her 101st birthday. She had been born at Chatham Barracks where her own father, Frederick Letchford (1806-1887) was a colour sergeant with (according to the *Sevenoaks Chronicle*) 'the old 50th regiment, known as the 'Blind Half Hundred' (a forerunner of The (Queen's Own) Royal West Kent Regiment). He had been born in Sevenoaks in the house which eventually became a pub, The Halfway House, and at one point, home to Charlie Draper *(see Part 3)*.

~

Part Five

SHADOW OF THE SOMME

Sevenoaks Men at the Somme

The Battle of the Somme, which lasted from 1st July 1916 until November the same year, would claim the lives of many local men.

The battle began in the morning of 1st July 1916. On that first day there were 57,470 casualties, of whom 19,240 men were killed. Five men – three officers and two privates – all from Sevenoaks, were killed on that day: Captain George Henry Heslop (Middlesex Regiment), Temporary Lieutenant Edouard H A Goss (The Buffs), Second Lieutenant Geoffrey Harrison (Machine Gun Corps)and Privates Jack Lewis and Leonard Bowles (Royal West Kent Regiment). Other casualties followed in the weeks ahead. Many, like Jack and Leonard, were from the ranks of the Royal West Kent Regiment.

A service was held at the grave of Private
Alfred Hope on the centenary of his death

Two of the men wounded were repatriated and died of their wounds at home. George Bernard Taylor (buried at Greatness Cemetery) and Alfred Hope (buried in the churchyard at St Lawrence, Seal Chart) were both privates in the Royal West Kent Regiment.

From mid-1916 the *Sevenoaks Chronicle* carried a weekly Roll of Honour, with photos of those missing, wounded or killed. It was impossible to be unaware of the human cost of the war, which affected every resident in some way. Many townspeople also watched the news and films at the local cinemas.

In December 1916, the *Chronicle* reported that:

> *All the first part of the week many persons have had to be refused admittance as the hall has been thronged by people to witness the official pictures of 'The Battle of the Somme'. No picture has bought home to the public heart and mind what our boys are having to endure more impressively and vividly than this picture.*

Cobden Road, part of the mid Victorian expansion to provide homes for the working classes of Sevenoaks in the St John's area, endured unusually high losses amongst the men who grew up there, with many of these sustained on the Somme battlefield.

The Stevens brothers, Allan and Harry, both of 6th Battalion of the Royal West Kent Regiment, had grown up at 2, Cobden Road. Allan had written to the *Kent Messenger* in January 1916 from the trenches where he served with the Lewis gun section:

> *Sir, - Being an inhabitant of Kent, do you think one of your readers would kindly send us a football?*
>
> *It is hard to get a football out here, and a game after the boys have come out of the trenches livens things up.*

Allan, who was killed at the Somme on 3rd July 1916, and his brother, Harry (killed on 7th October 1916), would have known George Taylor (no. 4), Fred Gilks (no. 18) and Jack Lewis (no. 5), all of 7th Battalion, from Cobden Road. Fred Gilks wrote home from the trenches of the Somme in July 1916 and described how Jack Lewis had been hit by a piece of shell as they occupied trenches that had been captured:

> *He turned to me and said: 'I am done for Fred'.*

**Private Jack Lewis, who was killed
in front of his friend and neighbour**

Fred Gilks was killed less than two weeks after his friend and on the same day as Lawrence Bowles, whose mother resided on Cobden Road. All are remembered on the Thiepval Memorial.

Ralph Pattenden formerly of 22, Cobden Road, also served with the 8th Battalion Royal West Kent Regiment, following several years' service with the Territorials. He survived, but needed to walk with a stick for the rest of his life. His brother, Tom, an upholsterer in the fledgling motor car business, joined the 13th Battalion, the London Regiment, arriving in France on 4th November 1914. Tom was killed at Aubers Ridge on 9th May 1915. His body was never found. Their brother George served with the 19th Battalion, the Canadian Expeditionary Force and survived the war to return to his new home in Toronto

These men were from a close knit local community and bound together by membership of many social networks. They joined up, trained, fought, and in many cases, died together. Back home, their families hoped for the best and waited for news.

The Thiepval Memorial, designed by Sir Edwin Lutyens, was unveiled in 1932. The memorial commemorates British and South African forces who lost their lives in the Somme sector before 20th March 1918 who have no known grave. Eighteen Sevenoaks men are remembered at Thiepval, their names inscribed on its panels. Other Sevenoaks men who died at the Somme and whose bodies were recovered are buried in the cemeteries of the Commonwealth War Graves Commission.

Saved by his Pocket Watch

George Marshall is one of the Sevenoaks men remembered on the town War Memorial and one of several who had lived on Buckhurst Avenue in the centre of the town. George emigrated to Australia in 1912 with his friend Arnold Jarvis. Both had previously been pupils at the Lady Boswell's school and sailed for a new life together on board the *Ionie*. Another Sevenoaks ANZAC, Kenrid Davey, was also on board and they were perhaps known to each other. George Marshall died from wounds sustained, according to a report in the *Sevenoaks Chronicle* of 27th July 1917 by:

> *...the accidental bursting of a bomb. Deceased, who left Sevenoaks for Australia about five years ago, joined the Imperial Force last year. In April last, he was married at Kensington and afterwards spent some days in Sevenoaks. Private Marshall is a brother-in-law of Mrs Marshall, whose husband is with the colours in Mesopotamia. Another brother of Private Marshall's is serving in France whilst Mrs Marshall has seven brothers in the army, the eldest of whom has been a prisoner of war in Germany since the battle of Mons, in which he was wounded.*

Harry Marshall was one of the brothers mentioned and served with the Army Service Corps in Mesopotamia. Harry, who before the war had worked for the firm of E.J. Payne, grocers, was himself mentioned in the *Chronicle* when he was hospitalised as a result of an accident. He later made a full recovery. Harry served as a Verger at St Nicholas church and died in 1937 aged 58.

The other brother mentioned in George's obituary, John, known as Jack, was 29 and was working as a gardener at the Royal Crown Hotel in Sevenoaks, when he enlisted under the Derby Scheme in December 1915. He served with the Royal West Kent Regiment. Initially at home with 9th Battalion, he was transferred to 8th Battalion in June 1916 and saw action with them in the Somme sector.

Harry Marshall's delivery van, parked in Buckhurst Avenue

Jack was wounded in early 1918 and invalided home to England to recover before returning to action. Later in the August, the *Sevenoaks Chronicle* carried a news report detailing how Jack had again been wounded. As the paper noted,

> *This is the second time that he has been wounded and but for a remarkable circumstance his wound on this occasion would undoubtedly have been fatal. It appears that in returning to France, after recovering from his previous wound, he purchased a watch at Folkestone, which he was wearing when struck for a second time. The bullet passed clean through the watch, which broke its force, before it entered his body, and so saved his life. It is also a notable coincidence that the second wound was exactly on the same spot as the first.*

Jack survived the war and returned to civilian life in January 1919, re-joining his wife, Ellen, at their home in Victoria Road, Sevenoaks.

Jack Whyntie MC

Cyril John 'Jack' Whyntie was an early recruit to Kitchener's Army and had a successful career throughout the war. Clearly earmarked as a promising recruit, his bravery was to win him the Military Cross in 1918. Jack's career demonstrates how the army came to promote men from the ranks to become officers, on merit, as the war progressed, in contrast to the normal practice of commissions being reserved for, and in the past purchased by, the upper classes.

Jack was born on 5th October 1894 in Kentish Town, London, to William Whyntie (1860-1948) a draper originally from Scotland, and his wife, Annie Frances (1867-1938).

By 1901 the family were living in Sevenoaks at 118, High Street. That year's census shows William working as a draper's manager and living with his wife, sons Jack and Fred, and daughter, Olive. Thirteen servants were also listed as residing at the premises.

By 1911, Jack was listed as an apprentice draper and the family now included two other daughters, Doris and Kathleen. Including servants and a companion to his wife, William Whyntie's sizeable home of fourteen rooms housed fifteen people, including the appropriately named Bertha Draper, sister of Frank Draper who was killed in 1917, and Charlie Draper, see page 88.

Whyntie & Co. in the High Street, Sevenoaks

The family were Wesleyans and William Whyntie often preached and involved himself in church business. Jack had been educated at Avenue House School, Sevenoaks, followed by the Judd School in Tonbridge. After leaving he had been apprenticed as a draper to Frank East of Tonbridge. Like many Sevenoaks men, shortly after the outbreak of war he enlisted at Tunbridge Wells on 4th September 1914 where he was assigned to 7th Battalion Royal West Kent Regiment. His papers show that he was 5' 10¾" tall with grey eyes, brown hair and a fresh complexion.

Sergeant Jack Whyntie
Royal West Kent Regiment

By the time Jack was sent to France with his battalion in July 1915 he had been promoted from lance corporal to corporal, lance sergeant and then sergeant. As a sergeant in 7th Royal West Kent Regiment, Jack saw action in the early days of the Somme and was present at the capture of Trones Wood, where three other Sevenoaks men, Fred Gilks, Lawrence Bowles and James Pettitt, all in Jack's battalion, lost their lives on 13th July 1916.

Jack Whyntie's records show that he remained at the Front until February 1917 when he returned home for four months. Perhaps it was during this period of leave that he sat for local photographer, Henry Essenhigh Corke, whose family firm was situated at 39 & 43, London Road. The Essenhigh Corke studio had offered free photographs to serving men. Many locals, as well as men who were stationed in the town, took advantage of the offer. Years later, over five hundred glass plate negatives were found in the former studio, which are now cared for by the Kent History and Library Centre, Maidstone.

In 1917 while still a serving sergeant in B Company of the 7th Royal West Kent Regiment, Jack applied for a temporary commission, which he received in the June, being gazetted as temporary Second Lieutenant Whyntie in 8th Battalion East Surrey Regiment. Thus he became a 'temporary gentleman'.

A few months later in October 1917, the *Sevenoaks Chronicle* reported that Jack had been wounded:

> ...*in the big advance, last Friday, October 12th. Going over the top - during which operation all his senior officers were hit - it fell to Lieut. Whyntie's lot to lead his company on in the advance until he, too, was hit by shrapnel some distance on. Lt. Whyntie is now lying in a hospital at the Base, suffering from shrapnel wounds in the thigh.*

The incident was mentioned in the battalion war diary:

> *The barrage started at Zero mins four minutes by Brigade time, and appeared fairly intense, but machine gun fire was immediately opened from guns posted close to our tape, which was not touched by the barrage at all. Second Lieutenant C Whyntie, the sole remaining Officer of 'D' Company, was wounded at once...*

In its November 23rd edition the *Chronicle* was able to report that Jack had sufficiently recovered to be able to rejoin his regiment.

On 4th April 1918, Jack was again injured, this time at Villers-Bretonneux on the Somme. Once again the *Sevenoaks Chronicle* reported news of his injury, stating that on this occasion he had been wounded by a bullet in the arm. Jack was sent back to England where he was treated at the 5th Southern General Hospital before being transferred to a convalescent home for officers. By June 1918 a Medical Board concluded that he had regained perfect movement in his shoulder and was fit for general service.

Later that year, by now serving as Acting Captain Whyntie, he was involved in an action for which he subsequently received the Military Cross. According to the citation (*London Gazette*, 4th October 1919), the award was:

> *For conspicuous gallantry and leadership near Ronssoy on the 18th September, 1918.*

He held his company well together in the dense mist and kept them straight on their objective. Owing to the failure of troops in front to take the Green Line the company soon found itself in the front line and met with heavy machine-gun fire. He at once extended his company and pushed on, thereby gaining two thousand yards of ground and reaching the Green Line.

**Captain Jack Whyntie
in the East Surrey Regiment**

After the Armistice, Jack continued to serve, for a time in the army of occupation. Then he returned to the family business where he became a director and settled in Sevenoaks with his wife, Helen, and two children, Barbara and Brian. A popular businessman, local resident and a keen follower of cricket, he was often seen watching matches on the Vine, which overlooks the War Memorial.

An advert for Whyntie & Co, *Sevenoaks Chronicle*, 1922

Jack Whyntie was taken ill suddenly when preparing to close the shop one Thursday evening in 1935 and died of meningitis on his 41st birthday on the following Saturday 5th October. He was buried in Greatness Cemetery.

Frederick Whyntie

His brother Fred, who had served as an air mechanic during the war, survived him by only two years. He died in 1937, followed the year after by their mother, aged 71. William Whyntie, the patriarch of the family, lived on until 1948 when he died aged 88 and was survived by his daughters and grandchildren.

The Davey Family

Kenrid Davey was one of many men from the Sevenoaks area who had emigrated to Australia and New Zealand before the outbreak of war.

Kenrid Horace Davey served with the New Zealand Rifle Brigade

Kenrid was born in Riverhead in late 1888, the son of David Davey (1853-1927) and his wife, Elizabeth, known as Lizzie (1853-1929). The 1891 census shows the family resident on Chipstead Lane with David working as a plumber and painter; Kenrid was one of six children then at home. By 1901, the family were living at *The Old School House* in Chipstead.

Kenrid emigrated to New Zealand on 4th January 1909, sailing Third Class from London to Port Chalmers on the *Kumara*. Kenrid's service records show that he was working as a butcher when he enlisted and was 5'4 tall, weighing 155 pounds. He gave his next of kin as his father who by then was living at Saint William's Villa, Dunton Green. His nearest relative in New Zealand was his older sister, Phyllis.

He embarked from Wellington on 9th October 1915 as a Rifleman in 1st Battalion, New Zealand Rifle Brigade bound for Suez and served in Egypt for the remainder of 1915 before leaving for the Western Front in April 1916. The New Zealand Division spent three months guarding a 'quiet' sector of the front line at Armentieres before they moved south to the Somme, where they joined that battle in early September 1916. The following year he was wounded in his left arm by a shell on 10th September 1917 at Ypres during the Battle of Passchendaele, and was invalided to England two weeks later.

His papers show a largely exemplary service record with just three disciplinary incidents: being AWOL for 2 hours in November 1916 (lost 14 days pay), trotting a horse on a cobbled road in January 1917 (lost 7 days pay) and for being without his helmet in March 1917 (lost 8 days pay).

Kenrid returned to New Zealand and died in 1968. His brother, Sidney Charles Davey (1894-1974), also served, having enlisted on 29th August 1914 and joined the Royal Engineers. He was commissioned as lieutenant with 11th Battalion The Liverpool Regiment at the end of 1916 and transferred to the Tank Corps in November 1917. That same month he was Mentioned in Dispatches.

Sidney Charles Davey

Several cousins of Kenrid and Sidney had also lived in the Sevenoaks area and fought during the war, including Horace James Taylor, a cousin through their mother's sister, Emma, who had married Alfred Taylor.

Horace Taylor was born in Sevenoaks on the 26th December 1895. His father, Alfred, would have been well known in the town as a harness and saddle maker. The 1911 census shows the family living at 50-52 London Road (known as *Belgrave House*) with Horace and his younger brother Alfred listed as being at school and their older sister, Millicent, recorded as an assistant school teacher.

**Horace James Taylor who played first class
cricket for Kent after the war**

Both attended Sevenoaks School as day boys; according to the *Sennockian* (1922) he left the school in 1912 and became a bank clerk.

Horace enlisted in late August 1914 when he was 19, joining the West Kent Yeomanry. He saw service with them at Gallipoli and in Egypt before going on to serve in Palestine and France. He served as a private, holding the rank of corporal for two brief periods. By June 1918 Horace had returned to England to attend a cadet course. He spent the remainder of the war working at the Larkhill Reception Camp in Wiltshire.

His brother, Alfred, also saw service having joined the 2nd Battalion London Regiment on the outbreak of war. He was transferred to the 13th Battalion West Riding Regiment in 1916. Both brothers survived the war.

Horace was known for his interest in and talent for cricket, first displayed at school when he played in the First XI 1910 – 1912. He was good enough to play for his county and appeared for the Kent side in twelve matches from 1922. He married Doris Austin in Tonbridge in 1935 and lived on until 1961.

Horace and Alfred's sister, Millicent, married their former fellow pupil, Arthur Thompson (son of the Sevenoaks Post Office Superintendent), who was also a former pupil of Lady Boswell's school.

Arthur was a captain attached to 10th Battalion King's Own Yorkshire Light Infantry when he was killed later on 25th September during the Battle of the Somme in an attack on Gird Trench. According to Second Lieutenant F R Parker, who wrote to Arthur's widow:

It grieves me to tell you of your husband's death in action on the 25th. Whilst gallantly leading his company to the assault, he was shot through the head; his death was instantaneous, so it was impossible for him to leave a message. Although he had only commanded his Company for a few weeks, in that short time, he had won the hearts of officers and men and the few that are left join me in sympathising with you in your very sad bereavement. Tommy, as we called him, was a great pal of one out here. Perhaps you will remember me meeting you in Newcastle? Please excuse me writing any more just now, as it upsets me to think about the last few days; but if you care to write to me, I shall only be too glad to write a little later.

His obituary in the *Sevenoaks School Quarterly* speaks of '*his young wife, whose courage under her cruel loss has taught us all a lesson of endurance and faith*'. Arthur's brother, Sidney Ernest Thompson, had died on 25th September 1915 at the Battle of Loos.

~

Part Six

HOME FRONT

Mrs Hodgson's War

The Hodgson family lived on Buckhurst Avenue in Sevenoaks. The 1911 census shows head of the family, John Watson Hodgson (1849-1919) a general labourer employed by the Urban District Council, and his wife, Eliza Thirza Hodgson (1864-1949) living at 7, Buckhurst Avenue with their three sons: John Watson and Charles Joseph, who are both working as dairymen, and their brother Ernest William, who was still at school.

Ernest, sat front far right and Charles, sat next to Rev Curteis,
4th right, middle row, St Nicholas Church

Eliza Watson kept a notebook throughout the war. More a commonplace book than a diary, it records the events of family life and information about her sons when they were in the army. It also includes notable events such as the death of people she knew, such as neighbour

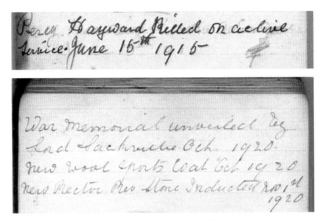

Extracts from Eliza's diary

Percy Hayward, who was killed in 1915 and is remembered on the town War Memorial, to the unveiling of the memorial itself in 1920.

All three sons served with the forces during the war, Ernest with the Household Battalion Life Guards, Charles with the Royal Engineers and John with the Middlesex Regiment.

Ernest Hodgson, 3rd row down, 5th from right

By the time of his enlistment, Ernest had become a printer, employed by renowned local firm J.Salmon of Sevenoaks. He sustained a gun shot wound to his right arm in May 1917 and was wounded again in October 1918.

John Watson senior appears to have suffered from poor health toward the end of his life. His son John appeared before the Military Tribunal to seek exemption in 1916 because, as

Ernest Hodgson in Buckhurst Avenue, Sevenoaks

the *Sevenoaks Chronicle* recorded, his two brothers had joined up and *'his mother being weak had to give occasional attention to his bed-ridden father'*. The paper noted that the tribunal treated him sympathetically, causing John to exclaim *'I thank you gentlemen'*, *in a manner that conveyed the idea that the result was very favourable'*.

Eliza Hodgson also featured in the local papers during the war but for very different reasons, being a key witness in the trial of a deserter, an event she noted in her diary. Both the *Chronicle* and the *Kent Messenger* reported the trial of William Ross, a private in the Royal Sussex Regiment. Ross was accused of stealing from Eliza, and a Mrs Nellie Flegg of Seal in April 1917.

At the initial hearing before the court in Sevenoaks, Ross was accused by Eliza Hodgson. She stated that he had called upon her and asked that he be put up for four days, saying that he had four days leave in order to visit a wounded pal in the Cornwall Hall hospital. He told her that he had been wounded in the Dardanelles and in France. According to the paper:

She allowed him to stay and he left without returning, after asking her to get her bill ready by the time he came back. She afterwards missed a silver watch chain, and on a visit to the Police Station, identified a gold ring and Treasury note case, which were there as her property. She had also missed some cap badges and soldiers' buttons.

Ross had then made his way to Seal where he had sought lodging with Nellie Flegg. Mrs Flegg gave evidence that Ross had told her he was with the Army Service Corps and had come from Bromley to Seal to *'be with his young lady'*. According to the news report:

At his request she allowed him to remain two days, and he had several meals there. When he disappeared, the money was missing from the mantelpiece.

After the police were alerted, he was apprehended in a general shop on the Otford Road. Ross told the police that he belonged to the Army Service Corps and was stationed at Bromley, stating *'I left there yesterday morning and have no pals'*. Taken by the police back to Seal he managed to escape for a short while before he was captured and identified by Mrs Flegg, explaining his attempted escape by saying *'I thought I had a good sporting chance of getting away'*. Once in custody he admitted that he was not a corporal despite wearing corporal's stripes and two gold wound stripes on his sleeves. At the hearing:

Ross made a statement on oath that he joined 14th Battalion Royal Sussex Regiment when it was first formed and went through the usual training, until they reached a depot at Codford. A draft of 300 men was there asked for to make up the 11th and 12th battalions of the Royal Sussex. In the hopes of getting across the sea quicker he volunteered for that draft and was sent to 12th battalion at Witney. With that battalion he went through further training and at the critical moment of the Brigade being ordered overseas the hut he was in was taken with measles. After isolation he found himself left with others on details. This disheartened him. He eventually found himself back with 14th Battalion, tried hard by volunteering for various drafts, but was not fit. He then lost heart and deserted.

William Ross was remanded in custody and sent for trial at the West Kent Quarter Sessions in Maidstone where he pleaded guilty to the four charges of stealing and incurring debts under false pretences. Ross admitted other offences. The *Chronicle* reported that:

Prisoner now asked to be handed over to the Military Authorities so that he might be sent to France but he was sentenced to six months' hard labour, the court leaving it to the Military Authorities to take what steps they might deem advisable.

What became of William Ross is unknown but all three Hodgson brothers survived the war. John Hodgson senior died in 1919, while his widow lived on until 1949. John and Eliza are buried, together with some of their children who had once sung in the church choir, in the churchyard at St Nicholas.

Women of Sevenoaks at War

Local women, from all walks of life, made a significant contribution during the war. They replaced the absent men in a broad range of occupations, from shop work (at E.J. Payne, the grocer's, only one male member of staff remained after 1916), to toiling in the Women's Land Army. Other women volunteered at the War Supply Depot, at 36, High Street, where they gathered to make clothing and hospital dressings. This work continued after the Armistice to support prisoners of war and the wounded. Appeals were also made to provide for refugees in Europe.

Marjorie Crosbie Hill took on an active role during the war. Born in Sutton, Surrey, in 1887, Marjorie was the daughter of William Samuel James Hill (1845-1915) and his wife

Elizabeth Mary Crosbie (1847-1908). William and Elizabeth had married in Islington in 1871. By 1891 they had moved to Sevenoaks, where William became a prominent resident and Justice of the Peace. The couple were recorded in that year's census living at *The Red House*, once the home of Francis Austen, an uncle of Jane Austen, and now the premises of local solicitors, Knocker & Foskett. The census shows Marjorie at home with five siblings, a governess and three servants. Later the family moved to 50, High Street. By 1911 Marjorie was living with her widowed father at 2, South Park. During the war, Marjorie, who was a Christian Scientist, worked organising and running canteens and clubs for workers at the munitions factories, for the Young Women's Christian Association. She was awarded the OBE for this war work in early 1918 and she sat for her portrait at around that time.

Marjorie Crosbie Hill

Marjorie's niece, Jane Ashmore, recalled:

My aunt, at one time, lived next door but one to the old Post Office on return from running two kitchens for munitions workers, for which she was decorated. After World War Two, she built herself a house in Burntwood Road, called Tussocks, (her tiny little beech hedge is now huge). Also, she was a well known golfer, belonging to the Knole Club (where she was Lady Captain in 1925 and 1930).

Marjorie later lived at Stone Street near Sevenoaks and died aged 80, in 1967. Her elder sister, Barbara, had married Sir James Masterton Smith, who was private secretary to successive First Lords of the Admiralty, including Winston Churchill.

Jane Ashmore's brother and Marjorie's nephew, Philip Sydney Crosbie Hill, was born during the war in 1917. He was in India, tea-planting in Assam when the Second World War broke out, and immediately applied for service in the Indian Army. He was an Officer Cadet, undergoing training in the Royal Bombay Sapper and Miners when he was killed in a motor accident in 1941. He is remembered on the Sevenoaks War Memorial.

Another local woman, Gladys Chapman, lived in the St John's area of Sevenoaks and was honoured for an act of bravery during the war.

According to a news report in the *Chronicle* on 31st January 1919, Gladys lived at 3, Barrack Corner, and during the war, worked at the Kings Norton Metal Factory at Abbey Wood. About 7000 workers were employed there during the war, most based in temporary huts. Shell and cartridge cases were made in Birmingham then assembled and loaded at the Abbey Wood Factory, next to Woolwich Arsenal.

Gladys Evelyn Chapman

Gladys was on duty when a fire broke out in the factory, caused by a spark from a machine igniting some cordite.

> *The outbreak spread to a stack of aerial bullets, and but for the energies of Miss Chapman might have become much more serious. Miss Chapman first filled pails with water, which were poured on the cases, which were smouldering; then when the foreman threw off the corrugated iron covering to get at the burning wood with hose pipes, she threw the sheets to one side. This done, she secured a small hose and played on the fire, although all through these operations the bullets were exploding and flying in all directions, making the undertaking at once extremely dangerous and alarming.*

Gladys was rightly recognised for her bravery and attended a ceremony in Brighton, where she was presented with her medal by Lord Leconfield, Lord Lieutenant of Sussex as a *'recognition of coolness and courage displayed by her, in face of great danger'*.

Although her award was credited as the OBE, it was actually a Medal of the Order of the

British Empire, which was awarded to over two thousand people from 1917 until 1922 when it became the Medal of the Order of the British Empire for Meritorious Service (usually referred to as British Empire Medal or BEM).

Rationing and Wartime Hardships

As the war progressed, life became increasingly difficult on the Home Front. With a prolonged German U-boat campaign reducing supplies and poor harvests at home, food prices rose and people were encouraged to reduce their consumption and urged not to panic buy. Fixed prices were imposed for essentials such as butter and sugar before rationing of key foodstuffs was introduced in 1918. The shortages naturally affected Sevenoaks and the Council was forced to take a more interventionist approach.

Prices increased for a range of goods, services, and foodstuffs, including petrol, which was rationed from July 1916 and doubled its cost. Overcrowding on local buses was one consequence of this policy.

The cost of living continued to rise with matching calls for a stricter national economy. Local papers had to adapt to the rising costs of paper and production and the *Chronicle* changed its format in October 1916 after becoming part of the *Kent and Sussex Courier*, having seen many of its staff leave to join to fight. The price of the *Chronicle* increased in March 1918 and readers were encouraged to share their copies with their neighbours.

From January 1917 railway services were curtailed further. Trains from Otford to Sevenoaks were discontinued and Bat and Ball Station (the first train station in Sevenoaks, opened in 1862) was closed to passenger traffic. The closure of the Otford line released eleven men for potential military service.

By December 1916, the Council responded to the growing food shortages by establishing a committee to consider the question of thrift and food production, with a brief to review the cultivation of public land for growing of crops. The committee's report proposed that there was plenty of public land that could be utilised, including some of the recreation ground on Hollybush Lane, land below the bowling green, some gardens of various houses, and even two plots in the cemetery grounds at Greatness. The Committee asked for the power to purchase seed, manure and other essentials and proposed the distribution of any profits to local hospitals and charities. Eventually, the land at the cemetery was not used. Despite efforts to spare some of the recreation ground, the majority of the site, some seven acres, was eventually given up to cultivation.

In the middle of the debate, Cllr George Marshall, Chair of the Food Production Committee was outraged by the sight of men playing bowls at the recreation ground. *'It seems little less than a public scandal'*, he thundered in a letter to the *Chronicle*, *'and a slur on our town that men able to bowl should not devote themselves to some more beneficial and national work'*. Such a public criticism warranted a robust response and it was received in a letter to the paper from George Wood, the Hon. Secretary of the bowls club, in which he asserted that *'...every one of the members who were playing bowls on the day he mentions are, to my certain knowledge, doing his bit in the way of exceptional effort ...and in addition, are doing supplementary war duties, such as constabulary and V.T.C work'*.

Families struggled as the cost of living increased. In January 1917, the case was heard of two married women and a young boy, all of Redmans Place, who had been caught stealing what was known as 'cleft wood' from Knole Park. Cut tree tops from the park were given away freely but cleft wood, which was larger, was stacked for use on the Knole estate or sold in Sevenoaks. It was stated in court that Lady Sackville had appealed for leniency in the matter. Aware that the accused, Mrs Marsh, was the wife of the wounded Private Marsh, and Private Marsh having written to Lady Sackville, the defendants were all fined half-a-crown each, despite the magistrate's observation that all of the defendants deserved to go to prison at Maidstone.

Prices for laundry increased, as did those for beer. From January 1917 a pint of bitter cost 3d and 2½d for mild and bitter. The price of beer would be of great interest to many. It was reckoned that the population of the Sevenoaks licensing district was 24,972, with 57 ale houses and 36 beerhouses, or one to every 268 people. Beer prices were increased again in the April so that a pint now cost 5d.

The price of coal was fixed by the Council for domestic customers in January 1917, during one of the coldest winters on record. Local people could also collect their supply from the railway sidings to save money and avoid a delivery charge. Efforts were made to stockpile coal, with one local merchant stating that he was prepared to store 200 tons of coal on his wharf as an emergency stock not to be touched until *'the stock for the poor people for the winter supply is exhausted'*. Local residents were advised to try not to heat more than one room.

With limited supply and the rising cost of fuel, the local baths were an attractive alternative for many. Open from 8 am to 8 pm, a 'Special bath' with soap and towels cost 1s; first class bath with soap and towels 6d; second class baths without soap or towels 3d.

Maximum prices were introduced for basic commodities. The *Sevenoaks Chronicle* began to publish a weekly series of articles, *'Back to the Land'*, to encourage and guide local people to grow their own produce in their gardens and elsewhere.

In March 1917, some Godden Green residents hired land at Bo Petts from Lord Sackville to grow vegetables intended for sale to the poor at a cheap rate. Lord Sackville offered several acres of Knole Park for cultivation but this was declined by the Council because of the difficulties of fencing and other issues.

At St. John's Baptist Church, Archdeacon Dunkerley was clear that agricultural work on a Sunday was not a sin. With allotments and cottage gardens lying undug, the Archdeacon stated that *'Men and women could do field work on Sundays'* while still trying to safeguard the day and give an hour of it to God, *'the present shortages made such war work acceptable'*.

Women and children took the place of the absent men and undertook arduous work on the land, especially during harvest time. The Kent Agricultural Committee appealed for people to work on the land. Local women joined the Women's Land Army, which was used extensively in the county. Senior pupils from Bayham Road School volunteered to dig the allotments that had been left when their owners had enlisted. Licences were also granted by the Kent Education Committee to allow children aged 12 to 14 to work on the land. A hundred and nine children in the Sevenoaks Rural District were granted such licences in the period between 1st April until 11th October 1917, and fourteen in Sevenoaks Urban District.

As part of the campaign to encourage people to ration their diet voluntarily, King George V issued a proclamation to encourage people to reduce their consumption of bread. The

Kent and Sussex Courier noted in June 1917 that the proclamation had been read out every Sunday by the Rector.

Consideration was given to the protection of crops grown. Where land had been taken under the Cultivation Order, any trespass became an offence under the Defence of the Realm Regulations, and those found stealing or damaging their neighbour's crops were liable to a £100 fine or imprisonment. Allotment societies and Special Constables would keep an eye on allotments and land that fell outside of the Order. By the spring of 1918, over 250 allotments had been created on new land, yielding over 16 tons of potatoes and 20 tons of swedes. Some land was given over to the use of Council schools, to help interest children in growing their own food, and much of the produce was donated to the local VAD hospitals.

The *Chronicle* was clear that it was no good hoping that the town would be able to '*muddle through*'. Rigid economy of food supplies was necessary, especially while the '*submarine menace*' had not yet been conquered. The sacrifice being asked of townsfolk was small, argued the paper, compared to that of soldiers and sailors.

Local MP H.W. Forster also emphasised the gravity of the situation and the importance of the Food Economy Campaign, in a letter published in the *Chronicle* in April 1917:

> *I fear that there are many people who still do not understand how grave the food problem has become, especially as regards bread. The fact is that we cannot get enough for our full needs. We cannot get it because firstly, the crop of last year was a total failure, secondly, because there are not enough ships to bring what we want.*
>
> *The poor must have the first claim. For them bread is a necessity. Those who can buy other forms of food must do without bread as far as possible. And in every household, rich or poor, there must be no waste.*

Talks on food cultivation and cookery were given, including demonstrations of hay-box cookery and cooking with substitutes for flour. Promising to prove '*invaluable to housewives*' the importance was emphasised to attendees of restricting their other occupations and devoting their time instead to finding and making use of various bread substitutes, thus leaving the bread itself for those who could not afford the more expensive foods, or had not the time to prepare them.

The first communal kitchen in Sevenoaks opened in the St John's district, where the need was greatest in the town, at the end of May 1917. About 50 dinners of meat pie followed by rice pudding were served on the first day, with the menu changing throughout the week and including stew followed by date pudding, and rissoles and jam rolls. Each dish cost 2d. The majority of customers in the first week were children whose fathers were at the Front while their mothers were engaged in war work and unable to cook. The kitchen was closed for the summer holidays but reopened once school term restarted. More kitchens were later opened at other locations, including Lady Boswell's School and St Nicholas' Infant School, where 1d was charged for every meal.

A National Kitchen was later opened at the Club Hall by the Vine in March 1918 (the building was destroyed by a bomb in 1940) with nourishing food prepared and sold at reasonable prices. '*Customers should come early and bring dishes. Nothing carries well in paper*', wrote the Honorary Secretary of the National Kitchen Committee to the *Chronicle*. Offering dishes such as lentil pies, the kitchen initially opened for four days in the week but proved so popular that this was quickly increased to every day except Sunday. The *Chronicle* noted:

> It is interesting to notice that various classes of the community are realising the convenience, in a busy life, of being able to procure nourishing food already prepared and at reasonable prices.

Food waste would not be tolerated and the first prosecution came in June 1917 when Bernard Cox, manager of the Army Canteen at Wildernesse Camp, was charged with the alleged wilful waste of food for fit human consumption by ordering its disposal for the feeding of pigs, under contravention of the Defence of the Realm Act. In July 1917, the Food Inspector reported to the Council that he had been overcharged for rolled oats that he had purchased from a tradesman at St John's. It was decided that the trader would be warned rather than prosecuted as his was the first such case to be reported, but that future offenders would face the full benefit of the law.

The local Food Production Campaign continued to promote cookery demonstrations and food preserving, providing glass jars and 800 lbs of sugar for the purpose in April 1917. A hundred and twenty-eight applications were received, and after consideration, the sugar allowance was distributed between 43 households, with priority given to those with families. Sugar rationing was introduced nationally in 1918.

Soldiers billeted in the town offered help where they could, assisting farmers in the Sevenoaks district to gather in the hay crop. In July 1917, a policeman from London wrote to the *Kent Messenger* offering his services and that of three to four colleagues during their forthcoming holiday to help local farmers. Sevenoaks residents helped in other ways too. Jack Lewis of Cobden Road, whose son, Jack, had been killed at the Somme in July 1916, was reported to have helped preserve the corn crops of four local famers by having shot 219 wood pigeons in 1917 alone. By the spring of 1918, approximately 200 German prisoners of war were working on farms in Kent. Groups of five or more went out under escort but otherwise the farmers would call at one of five depots across the county to collect the men in the morning and return them in the evening. Nearer to home, at Riverhill, a group of German prisoners worked on the gravel pits there. The Rector called them 'a constant witness to the war'.

As the situation grew more serious, compulsory rationing was introduced by the government. First sugar, and then by April 1918, meat, butter, cheese, and margarine were added to the list.

On 2nd February 1918, the *Kent Messenger* reported that:

> Last week was by far the worst yet experienced in the Sevenoaks district for general shortage of supplies. The butchers had practically nothing to offer on Saturday morning, while most coming into the town to do their usual shopping found most of the butchers' shops closed. The cheaper kinds of fish were also conspicuous by their absence. The explanation being that there was practically no margin between the controlled sale price and the market price, so that with the cost of carriage the tradesmen stood only to lose

on their sales. …Little improvement occurred this week, and it is quite a rare thing to secure a joint although a little meat is on sale for the weekend. Naturally there has been a great demand for tinned meat, of which fortunately there has been a good supply.

The same month, a 'Mother of Six' wrote to the *Chronicle* to enquire whether it might be in the power of the Food Production Committee to *'enable the working people to get a joint occasionally?'*. She continued *'Remember we have no 'long stocking' to draw from, and are dependent on our husband's wages, and in the majority of cases do not get our housekeeping until Saturday morning'*. The author stated that it was impossible for her to buy her meat before the weekend without getting into debt, which she did not want to do. The mother, from Greatness, continued:

How strange it is to go shopping with over 30s now. Before the war, shopkeepers used to tempt us with all sorts of things; now one has to humbly ask as a favour for bare neces-sities, and occasionally the shopkeepers are far from civil and polite. We do not ask for favours to be shown us, but to be allowed to purchase (if we can) what we require and to be treated as human beings, not so much as cattle.

This opinion was supported by another correspondent in the paper's next edition. 'A Soldier's Wife' from Bat and Ball was glad that the previous writer had *'mentioned a growing evil, the manner in which tradesmen treat their customers – or rather would-be customers. Civility costs nothing and they should remember that our husbands and sons are fighting for them'*.

The Food Production Committee picked up on this issue and efforts were made to offer other foodstuffs, including fish and seafood, for sale at the Club Hall late on Saturday after-noons.

Rationing continued for the duration of the war and beyond with some items, such as butter, officially restricted until 1920.

The Threat from the Air

The war brought a new and terrifying phenomenon, that of enemy aircraft, with Zeppelin seen above Sevenoaks, often en-route for targets in London.

Air raids became a growing concern and instructions were issued to local people. The *Chronicle* carried a plea from the Postmaster General for the public not to use telephones during and immediately after a raid. Local store S. Young and Son offered dark blinds and casement curtains which could be provided at 24 hours' notice for the required blackout.

The threat of enemy action from the air was perhaps bought home by the death of Percy John Brooks of Bradbourne Road, Sevenoaks, who was killed in an air raid whilst away from home on 13/14th October 1915 in the so-called 'Theatreland Raid'. This saw five Zeppelins ar-riving over the Norfolk coast from where they proceeded to London, dropping their bombs in the centre of the capital, near Charing Cross and striking the Lyceum theatre, resulting in a number of casualties. Percy's body was returned for burial at Greatness Cemetery.

In his memoir of the Great War for Children, the Rector wrote:

...big aeroplanes (Gothas) began to come across instead of 'Zepps' and some of you will remember the noise of the guns all around Sevenoaks as they fired at them. There were guns at Riverhill, and Ide Hill, and Knockholt, and Wrotham, and other places round, and they were always ready to fire. It was like a battle here in Sevenoaks when the guns were firing. The streets of Sevenoaks were kept quite dark. No lights were allowed to be seen, except the great searchlights all over the sky; and when a raid was going on all the electric lights went out in the town, and the gas was lowered. Once in church on a Sunday evening, while we were having service, the electric light went out, and I had to close the service and the people went out in the dark. The German aeroplanes had come, and were passing over us. Through all the war we never had a bomb dropped actually in Sevenoaks, and for that we have to be thankful. Our own aeroplanes were constantly flying over Sevenoaks.

Sometimes during the day, and night too, you could hear the guns in Belgium and France if the fighting was near the coast. Down in the Weald the sound was much clearer than up here, and when a big battle was going on the deep thud of the guns was very plain.

Colonel Rogers of Riverhill House just outside of Sevenoaks, recorded in his diary on 24th September 1916

Nimmie (his daughter) *woke me at 1pm having heard a Zeppelin, we went out, but seeing nothing went back to bed. One was brought down in Essex, if we had gone up the hill we should have seen it.*

1st October
Zeppelin warning at 10pm, I went to Knole at 11-40 first gun fired to NW. 5 minutes later a great flare and a red burning Zepp fell from a cloud. This one fell at Potters Bar.

On 6th October 1916, the *Chronicle* reported that:

The burning Zeppelin aroused much excitement in the town, with many cheering.

The paper noted that *'at the first moment the light of the fire was seen it looked something like a bright red signal lamp'.*

Because of the light restrictions, stores such as the Furniture Town Sale Rooms on London Road urged their customers to do their shopping by daylight, otherwise *'The public will be unable to see after dark the unusual display of bargains in our windows'.* Enforcement of these restrictions was taken seriously and reports of prosecutions and fines were well publicised. In October 1916, three local residents were fined at Sevenoaks Police Court. Harriet Scarborough of 87, London Road was prosecuted for failing to act when a policeman told her to lower the light or put up a blind. Mrs Scarborough was, apparently, a repeat offender, and her failure to comply on this occasion led to a fine of £2.

Henry Herbert Hill, a baker and confectioner at Dartford Terrace, St John's, who was to lose his son later that year in Egypt, was fined for allowing a light to shine from a side window and be visible in Hollybush Lane. The chairman had no time for this case, warning *'It* is absolute madness to show these lights. If a bomb missed you, it might hit your neighbours'.

The *Chronicle* made its own view clear, stating that inconvenience was not an acceptable plea:

What would it profit an individual or a community if in the attempt to save a baker's batch his establishment was blown to atoms with others and their occupants lost their lives?

Herbert Hill's bakery stood on the corner
of Dartford Road and Hollybush Lane

One of the Special Constables charged with enforcing the regulations added wearily that 'A *little more care would materially help us, and save much wear and tear of door knockers and official lungs!'.*

Neither were the military nor other organisations exempt from prosecution. Both the YMCA and the army were prosecuted and fined during the war.

Many residents resented the total blackout required and numerous letters were received by local papers on the matter. Correspondents felt that the total darkness imposed was unnecessary and ran the risk of causing accidents and serious harm to local residents simply trying to go about their normal business.

They would have to wait until the end of hostilities for the lighting restrictions to be lifted and the town to emerge from the literal darkness of the war.

Wartime Christmases

In 1914, the popular firm of S.Young and Co. used its regular advertisement in the *Kent Messenger* to promote its Grand Bazaar, setting the tone by asking the question: *Christmas as usual? Why not?*

> *There are thousands of soldiers and sailors to whom Christmas will mean more this year than ever before. There are thousands of children for whom Christmas would be poor indeed if the old customs were not kept up.*

With so many local men away and large numbers of Belgian refugees in the town, as well as wounded servicemen at the newly established hospitals, fundraising was the order of the day.

Entertainments for troops, refugees, and the wounded were held. Lord and Lady Sackville hosted a concert at Knole in aid of the St John's VAD hospital which their daughter, Vita, had helped establish. Held on the afternoon of 15th December, the concert featured some well-known artistes, including Miss Phyllis Dare and Miss Constance Collier. Children of the Knole estate workers were also invited to a Christmas tea on a Wednesday afternoon.

Patriotic Christmas cards like this were sent in 1914

The troops billeted in the town were not forgotten and the Territorials Christmas fund raised £167 17s 5d, which was distributed between 4th and 5th Loyal North Lancashires, 4th and 5th King's Own, the Army Service Corps, and the Army Medical Corps and Divisional Head-quarters. The remainder was given to the Soldiers' and Sailors' Families Association.

Letters sent home were regularly forwarded to the *Sevenoaks Chronicle* to be reproduced for popular consumption. In 1914 Private Ernest George Saxby of G Company 2/4th Battalion Royal West Kent Regiment wrote to local recruiting officer Captain H W Knocker. Saxby, of Seal Chart, near Sevenoaks, had joined the Territorials on 2nd November 1914.

Christmas at the Cornwall Hall hospital, 1916

I am pleased to say that I am quite enjoying myself in my new life. The fellows here are a very sociable lot. The food we have is very good indeed and I have no doubt Major Laurie looks after G Company as well as any.

Our 1st lieutenant is the Reverend Thompson's son, and our second lieutenant is Archdeacon Dunkerley's son of St John's.

I expect to get home for Christmas and I hope I shall as I have always spent it at home up till now. We have some very nice route marches of sixteen to eighteen miles and come home very tired, but full of fun. We have a football XI and are going to play for a cup and shield among the Companies. After all, army life is not all bad.

News sometimes arrived home from Sevenoaks men being held as prisoners of war. One such man was 20 year old Albert Hayward, the son of William, an old soldier, and his wife Jane, who resided at 13, Buckhurst Avenue, Sevenoaks. Albert was working as an apprentice printer before the war and enlisted in London in November 1914. He fought at Ypres with 2nd Battalion The Buffs, where he was taken prisoner in April 1915.

The *Chronicle* carried a report in January 1916 under the title *A Sevenoaks Soldier in Germany, Xmas in an Internment Camp*, which featured a postcard that Albert had written to his parents:

Just a hurried line to thank you for the two parcels which I received in quite good condition. I think I told you that the pudding was quite good, and that the cigars were quite nice and mild. I enjoyed my 'Xmas quite well under the circumstances. My chum and I had a tin of mutton chops, 'Xmas pudding, beef and vegetables, for dinner. Of course we managed to forget nuts, oranges, apples etc. the 'boss' gave us a bag containing 50 cigarettes, buns and lbs of apples; we also had a 'Xmas tree decorated up, and we were allowed one bottle of lager

Patients enjoying Christmas lunch at the Cornwall Hall, 1917

beer, which was half the dinner. I hope you all had a very enjoyable 'Xmas and New Year, and good weather, for we have had some heavy falls of snow lately, but it has changed to rain now. Please tender my thanks to the Rev J Rooker for the card he sent me of the Parish Church. I hope you are all as well at home as this letter leaves me - in the best of health.

Albert saw one more Christmas before he died as a result of his diabetes in October 1917. He is buried in the Niederzwehren Cemetery in Hessen, Germany. Albert and his brother, Percy, who was killed earlier in the war, are remembered on the family grave at St Nicholas' Church, Sevenoaks.

Throughout the war years, the *Chronicle* reported on how Christmas was spent in the local VAD hospitals, where staff and patients celebrated the festive season together. In 1916, the large ward at Cornwall Hall was decorated with holly and laurel. Another ward featured *'a model of a gigantic Zeppelin, with excellent models of aeroplanes in close proximity to it'.*

The paper printed a letter from A PATIENT, who outlined what he and his fellow patients had enjoyed:

On Christmas Day, after many of the nurses and patients had attended Divine Service at the Parish Church, there was an incessant round of festivities, commencing with a splendid dinner, served in the large ward (cooked at the Royal Crown Hotel, through the kind thoughtfulness of Mr Marshall). Crackers and flowers made the tables look inviting, but when the board was covered with turkeys, mince pies, plum puddings and dessert, the effect was greatly increased.

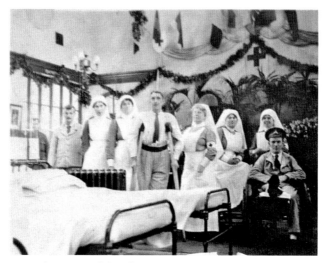

Boxing Day celebrations at the Cornwall Hall hospital

At St John's Hall hospital,

The festivities began in the early morning with the good old custom of Santa Claus, each man waking up to find a bulging sock in his bed; a surprise provided by the staff and much appreciated by the patients.

In the afternoon, after a typical Christmas tea, there was the stripping of a fine Christmas tree laden with gifts of all kinds, both for the staff and patients. A first-rate football from the nurses to the patients caused much applause as being a happy omen of future victories.

The Cornwall Hall hospital was still treating patients after the end of the war. This is Christmas 1918

In its 1918 Christmas editorial, the *Chronicle* noted that despite the still somewhat dimly lighted streets,

> *Sevenoaks has been wearing during the past week or so, a cheerier aspect. The Christmas of 1918 promises to carry with it some of the old-time gaiety. Peace on earth has a greater meaning than, perhaps, it ever had before.*

Part Seven

HISTORIC INSTITUTIONS

Sevenoaks School

Around 350 former pupils (known as Old Sennockians) enlisted during the course of the war, about 35 of whom were killed. George Heslop was the headmaster throughout the conflict and suffered, as many parents did, the loss of his son, Captain George Henry Heslop.

George Henry Heslop was one of the five Sevenoaks men who died on (or whose death was officially recorded as having occurred on) the first day of the Battle of the Somme on 1st July 1916. The battle, the launch of which was preceded by a week-long artillery bombardment, claimed over 19,000 lives on the first day. Other Sevenoaks men lost their lives during the course of the battle, which lasted until November 1916.

The 1901 census shows young George living with his father, and mother, Gertrude, at the School, with George's three sisters, Margaret, Evelyn and Faith.

George was later a pupil at Lancing College, where he was a member of the Officer Training Corps. He was also a keen cricketer, playing in the Cricket XI from 1911 to 1914 being Captain in 1913 and 1914. He topped the batting average in all his summer terms, scoring 981 runs in his time at Lancing, finishing the 1914 season with an average of 89. He was described by *Wisden* as being *'the most promising young all-rounder cricketer who had yet to appear in a first class match'*.

He won a place at Trinity College Cambridge in 1914 but did not take it, due to the outbreak of war, choosing to join the army instead. On the 11th September 1914 he enlisted at 24 St James Street, London as Private 433 in the Public Schools Battalion of the Middlesex Regiment.

Heslop was commissioned as a second lieutenant in the 16th Battalion on the 29th September 1914; was promoted to lieutenant on the 25th January 1915 and to captain on the 17th May 1915. He attended Staff College for a month and qualified as a first class instructor of musketry.

On the 1st July 1916, George was leading the men of D Company of 16th Battalion Middlesex Regiment. They reached their assembly positions by 3am and by 6.25am the British

George Henry Heslop, a skilled cricketer,
he became a captain in the Middlesex Regiment

artillery barrage had become intense as zero hour approached. At 7.20am the mine under the Hawthorn Ridge exploded and at 7.30am the British advance began. The Middlesex followed at 7.55am, D Company quickly formed up into ranks and moved forward.

As they crossed No Man's Land their ranks were swept by intense machine gun fire and men began to fall immediately. German artillery also joined the retaliation, focused on the front line and support trenches it added to the enormous casualties. The attack quickly faded under the weight of fire with the few survivors going to ground to seek cover. But most had

George Heslop's grave at the Hawthorn Ridge Cemetery No.1

died in the 200 yards between the British Front line and the edge of the Hawthorn crater, including George Heslop.

Heslop's family, at home at Sevenoaks School, received a telegram informing them of his death on 6th July. His devastated father mentioned his loss in a letter to a parent *'My boy was killed on 1st July in the first ten minutes of the great push. There is nothing to say. He had a duty to do and it was done'.*

George Heslop senior, headmaster of
Sevenoaks School throughout the war

Heslop's wife and daughters played their part in the war effort. Mrs Heslop was a lady caterer at the Cornwall Hall VAD Hospital from October 1914 and continued in the role for the duration of the war. Daughters, Margaret and Evelyn, nursed at Cornwall Hall (Margaret from September 1915 until January 1916; Evelyn from January 1915 until May 1916). Both women also assumed teaching duties at the school as the majority of the male staff left to enlist. Their sister, Gertrude, was a nurse in France.

Twelve year old pupil, Leslie White, wrote in March 1917:

As some of our old boys have won the Military Cross there is an extra holiday this afternoon…The news on the Western Front seems jolly exciting doesn't it?…Wednesday we had General French down here reviewing the troops in Knole Park…On Friday we had a little excitement from the air. It was only a few miles away and we could hear the engines quite distinctly…

Charles W R Knight (1884-1957) was one former pupil who received the Military Cross. A local resident, he enlisted in August 1914 and served in France first as a private in the Honourable Artillery Company. He applied for a temporary commission as an officer in May 1915, which was endorsed by George Heslop, as his former headmaster. The officer supporting his application wrote *'He has served with the HAC during the last 8 months and has proved himself a first class soldier. He should make a fine officer'.* He was commissioned as a second lieutenant and rose to acting captain in the Royal West Kent Regiment. A skilled marksman, he became known as 'Sniper Knight'.

Knight had a passion for wildlife, natural history, and falconry. In later life he became well-known for his exploits with his Golden Eagle 'Mr Ramshaw' and he appeared in a number of films. In 1915 he contributed an article to Country Life entitled '*Wildlife in the trenches*'.

He was later awarded the Military Cross '*For conspicuous gallantry in action. He displayed great courage and determination in organising an attacking party and securing his flank at a critical time. He set a splendid example throughout*'. (*London Gazette* 10th January 1917)

William Henry Burfoot of Chipstead, another former pupil, served as a second lieutenant with the Dorsetshire Regiment. He later transferred to the Royal Flying Corps and was killed in an accident when testing a new plane on 31st May 1918. According to the *Sevenoaks Chronicle* '*something went wrong with the engine, with the result that the deceased was pitched out and had his neck broken. The machine then caught alight and he was badly burned*'. William Burfoot was buried in the churchyard at St. Botolph's, Chevening, with members of the air force acting as pall-bearers. The Countess Stanhope attended the funeral.

Another Old Boy, Herbert George Brackley, served as a pilot in the Royal Naval Air Service. He was a flight lieutenant with No. 7 Squadron. Brackley was awarded the Distinguished Service Cross '*For conspicuously good work as pilot of a bombing machine. He has carried out twelve raids since 1st June 1916, mostly by night. On one occasion he returned with forty holes in his machine*' (citation in the *London Gazette*, May 1917).

Shortly after he was awarded the Distinguished Service Order '*in recognition of his services on the morning of 14th April 1917, when he carried out a raid on Bruges Harbour, with good results in spite of difficult conditions. Great credit is due to him for his persistence and determination. He also dropped bombs on Ostend seaplane base on the night of 3rd – 4th May 1917, making two trips*' (*London Gazette*, June 1917). He received the Croix de Guerre from the French Government in 1918 and was also honoured by the Belgian Government.

In 1918, on the formation of the Royal Air Force, he became the first commanding officer of 214 Squadron. Brackley, known as 'Brackles' survived the war and married Frida, daughter of Robert Mond of Combe Bank. He had a distinguished career in civil aviation until he returned to the RAF during the Second World War when he attained the rank of air commodore. He drowned in an accident in Rio de Janeiro in 1948.

The School celebrated the successes of its former pupils and mourned its losses. Ten Old Sennockians are named on the town War Memorial: Bernard G Bowles, Thomas Fishenden, Charles Hendry, George Heslop, Thomas Phelps, Henry Poland, Frank Robinson, brothers Arthur and Sidney Thompson, and Raymond White.

Later in the war, in November 1917, the Headmaster wrote to one boy's parents:

The war is very cruel. By our post yesterday I heard of the deaths of two more old boys. We schoolmasters have suffered. For though our boys are not of our blood they become very dear to us and something more than friends.

Life at the school continued, although the establishment was in decline, with Heslop senior heartbroken at the death of his only son. He stopped teaching in 1918 and a new headmaster arrived to take over in 1919.

Knole at War

Knole, the Sevenoaks seat of the Sackville family, has long played a role in the life of the town and did so during the First World War. Lord Sackville served with the army, seeing action in Gallipoli, Palestine, Egypt and France, while his wife was an ardent fundraiser for wartime charities. The estate also played a significant role as a military camp and training ground.

Lord Sackville, a colonel in the West Kent Yeomanry hurried away to join his men at camp in Canterbury once war had been declared. Jack Dinham, his coachman and groom at Knole, served with him, in a new capacity as his corporal groom.

Almost immediately, Knole was offered as an annex to the local hospitals and the Great Hall was turned into a convalescent home.

Gradually the thriving community of Knole dwindled as the men of the estate enlisted and left for training and abroad. More would be summoned by conscription.

Outwardly, Lady Sackville did what was expected of someone of her class and by the local community, from entertaining officers of the Yeomanry to dinner in the Great Hall at Knole and opening the house and gardens, to visiting wounded soldiers, and her efforts connected with fundraising for the war loan. All of this was dutifully done and equally dutifully reported by the local press. In 1918, Lady Sackville established her eponymous fund for Kent prisoners of war, which, within four months, was supporting 55 local men who were prisoners abroad, 20 of whom were from Sevenoaks.

The future 6th Lord Sackville, son of the then Lord's brother, Hon. Bertrand Sackville West, was a small boy when he wrote to King George V during the conflict, to ask plaintively:

> *'When will the War be over? I miss my daddy and having sugar on my porridge',* to which the King replied personally, *'I hope the War will be over soon and that your daddy will come back. I too miss having sugar on my porridge.'*

Lady Sackville, the boy's aunt, was not above writing her own letters to complain of the privations, as she saw them, inflicted by the war. She wrote, according to her daughter Vita's later memoir *'Pepita'*, to Lord Kitchener, to complain about the number of household staff being taken for the war effort. She expressed her horror at what she saw as the subsequent decline in standards, writing that she never thought she would see parlour maids at Knole.

Three of the men on the Sevenoaks War Memorial were employed at Knole before they enlisted. According to his obituary, William Robert Copper (1883-1917), a bombardier with 24th Siege Battery, Royal Garrison Artillery, had worked at Knole for six years before joining the army. He was a keen cricketer and played regularly for nearby Godden Green, where many of the workers from the estate lived and where he is also remembered on the village War Memorial.

Thomas Edmund Pattenden (1877-1918), a sergeant with 1/5th Battalion Royal West Kent Regiment, worked as a wicket porter at Knole, living on site with his wife, Florence, and their two children Doris and John. Thomas spent most of the war in India, where he died and was buried in Jubbulpore Cantonment Cemetery in 1918. His widow continued in his role as wicket porter at Knole until the 1930s.

Bombardier William Robert Copper worked on the
Knole estate for 6 years before joining up

Oliver Older (1878-1916) was born in Sevenoaks and, after working in London for some years, had returned home and was a groom at Knole before serving with the 6th Battalion, Royal West Kent Regiment. Oliver died of his wounds in October 1916 and is buried at Heilly Station Cemetery, Mericourt-L´Abbe, France.

A fourth man on the memorial, William Goss Hicks (1882-1917), was headmaster at the Lady Boswell School, and son of the butler at Knole, William Hicks senior.

In 1916, the *Kent Messenger* reported that before the war there had been 71 employees on the estate, now reduced to 52. The paper noted, perhaps generously, that when the Derby Scheme had been introduced, Lady Sackville *'did her best to get all the employees to attest, and all within age did so'.*

On 1st July 1916, in an article entitled *'The National Importance of Knole'*, the *Kent Messenger* reported the case of Adin Clifton Jeffery (1878-1940), works foreman at Knole, before the West Kent Appeal Tribunal. This heard the cases of men who were appealing against the decisions of their local tribunal. George Saer represented the Knole Estate for Lord Sackville with Mr Knocker, of the then well-known Sevenoaks solicitors, Knocker & Knocker.

According to the report, Jeffery had been in post for five years and his father had held it for 30 years before him. The tribunal heard that he had tried to attest under the Derby Scheme but had been rejected because of an enlarged heart. Jeffery's solicitor stated that he had attempted to go before a Medical Board but had been unable to get an appointment.

The National Importance of Knole

Before the West Kent Appeal Tribunal on Wednesday,

Mr. Geo. Saer, representing the Knole estate, Sevenoaks, for Lord Sackville, appealed for Adin Clifton Jeffery, aged 38, works foreman.

The appellant was legally represented by Mr. Knocker (Messrs. Knocker and Knocker, solicitors), and under examination said he had held his position for five years, and his father held it for 30 years. Knole House, of which he had acquired special knowledge, had 365 rooms, and its roof was some seven acres in extent. The drainage system was about 150 years old. Before the war there were 71 employees on the estate. They had been reduced to 52. At the outbreak of war Lord Sackville went with his regiment to Gallipoli, and fought through that campaign. He was now in Egypt. When Lord Derby's scheme was introduced Lady Sackville did her best to get all the employees to attest, and all within the age did so. He (appellant), on attesting, was told he had an enlarged heart, but received no certificate.

Mr. Knocker said Jeffery had applied to go before the Medical Board, but could not get an appointment.

How the *Sevenoaks Chronicle* reported the story

The tribunal heard that Knole contained 365 rooms and its roof covered approximately 7 acres, with, as Jeffery testified, 17 baths and 40 lavatories, as well as several sets of heating apparatus, all of which had to be kept in working order. Further evidence was given of the scale of Knole and the work required to maintain the estate:

...some part of the roof of Knole had to receive attention every day, and the antiquated drainage system required constant attention. In addition to the house, there were nine farms on the estate, two being in hand. Fifty tons of firewood per week were being cut for the troops, and about 7000 fir trees had been cut for the Government during the past eighteen months.

The case was made that no replacement would know the workings of the estate like the defendant:

It would not be possible for anyone to pick up in a few months the ramifications of the drainage system, of which the only plan was 150 to 200 years old, and that was useless, as there had been additions from time to time.

Mr Knocker emphasised the national importance of Knole and said that the appeal was not in Lady Sackville's interest, but for the nation.

Colonel Atkinson, military representative at the tribunal, suggested that the Medical Board were overworked and although he noted that it was only by a small majority that Jeffery had been allowed to appeal his case to this hearing, he was prepared to agree that Jeffery was doing essential work and, in view of his age, would not press for him to serve. Atkinson expressed his opinion that all the employees at Knole had done splendidly.

The court ordered that the case should stand over under regulations until Jeffery was called up when he would have seven days to appeal again.

Adin Jeffery continued to work at Knole until his death, aged 62 in 1940, when he was employed as steward. The *Sevenoaks Chronicle* noted in his obituary that he had been a keen member of the town Choral Society and sang in the choir of the Vine Baptist Church for nearly 40 years. He had died suddenly, collapsing in his chair, while going about his normal duties. According to the paper,

> *It was fitting to say that he loved the great house of Knole. It was a joy to him that he dwelt under its roof, and he found continual happiness in serving it, and the members of the family residing there, whom he honoured. Often he said that he hoped to end his days at Knole, and it was given unto him to continue his service to the last moment of his life within its walls.*

In a mark of the esteem in which he was held, Lord and Lady Sackville, Eddy and Bertram Sackville West all attended his funeral and sent flowers, as did Vita Sackville West.

The case of another Knole employee, Edwin Thomas Harding, aged 45, of Upper Park Lodge, Knole, who had been employed for two years, came before the Sevenoaks Tribunal in 1918. Again supported by Lady Sackville, on behalf of her husband, he appealed on the grounds of the risk to the house from fire breaking out. It was pointed out that:

> *with the exception of the butler, who was 68 years of age, he was the only man about the house during the day who understood the fire appliances.*

This case divided the Tribunal panel. The Chairman and one other felt that they had taken other men from Knole and that considering the treasures that were in the house they ought to give consideration to the appeal. Another panel member, Mr White, took the view that it would be a public scandal if they exempted him, because there were plenty of men engaged outside the house if they were wanted in case of fire and the local fire brigade could attend within five minutes.

Harding himself testified that he did everything that was necessary when a man's work was required and spent his whole time in the house, being the only one who understood the fire appliances and able to attend to them if he should be required.

A query as to whether there had been any attempt to replace him was met with the reply that there were now no men in the garden excepting very old men and boys. The gardeners now, in common with other head gardeners, had to dig instead of supervising.

It was proposed that two months exemption be given but an amendment was moved by Mr White and a fellow panel member that no exemption be given but that he should not be called for 56 days. This was carried by three votes to two, leaving Mr White to remark that

> *...he recognised that Knole was a sort of national treasure-house, but it was the larger national interests they had to study and that was the Army.*

The risk of fire in the house was a real one, as demonstrated in December 1918 when Lord Sackville's son-in-law, Harold Nicholson, was awakened by smoke and managed to raise the alarm and put out the blaze with the help of the night watchmen and tradesmen. The paper reported that the fire was thought to have been caused by an overheated hearth and

There is no doubt that Lord Sackville as well as his son-in-law had narrow escapes, the beam (that had caught fire) being the main support of his Lordship's bedroom floor.

Edwin Harding's son, Leonard Edwin (1899-1991), had served with the Royal Fusiliers from March 1917. The *Chronicle* reported in May 1918 that he had been missing since 24th April. However, Leonard Harding survived the war and long after, living to be 91.

The *Kent Messenger* carried news in March 1917 of how one former Knole gardener had been injured on service at home. Driver William Smith of the Royal West Kent Regiment, son of Mrs Smith of Godden Green, had been badly injured by a kick in the face from a mule at Kennington, near Ashford. According to the paper, his teeth were knocked out and his face so badly cut that it had to be sewn up.

Later that year, in September 1917, it was reported in the *'Our Boys'* column of the *Sevenoaks Chronicle* that Private John W Potter had made a surprise visit to his parents. Potter had worked with his father for five years in the Blacksmiths Forge at Knole and had joined the army in November 1916 aged 19. Putting his training to good use, he had been selected for *'flying machines repair work'* and was employed in the Royal Naval Flying Corps workshops.

Charles Tye of Godden Green was another member of the Knole staff, who had been employed as a tradesman before joining the Royal West Kent Regiment. According to the *Kent Messenger* in August 1918, Private Tye had been in France for about 15 months and his wife had just received word that he had sustained serious injuries to his shoulders, thigh and one of his legs, and was being treated in hospital.

Men from all parts of the Knole estate served during the war. Some would not return. The Tribunal records also offer a fascinating glimpse of how Knole, its owners and their remaining staff were perceived. They, like others in the town and across the country, were required to make sacrifices.

Though the War Office had taken many of the men from Knole, it was overreaching itself when William Reynolds of Back Lane, Godden Green, received his enlistment papers. Reynolds had been in the army in his younger days and had seen service in India. However, aged 67, the *Chronicle* reported that *'He treats the matter quite as a joke'*.

Sons of the Clergy

The vicars of Sevenoaks and the surrounding district took an active leadership role during the war. The daily life of the churches continued despite some unavoidable changes, such as the alteration of service times because of the evening curfew. They continued to minister to their congregations and to support all affected by the conflict; burying those who died of their wounds at home and comforting the bereaved. No congregation was immune from the effects of the war and many former members were now serving aboard. A Roll of Honour was compiled and kept in many churches. Vicars also played an active role in encouraging volunteering and recruitment drives. They spoke at many of the public meetings that were regularly held. In some cases, their wives did the same and spoke directly to the women of Sevenoaks. It was perhaps inevitable that many of their children served in the army, worked as chaplains or nursed, following in the example of their parents.

The Reverend Henry Percy Thompson officiated at St Mary's Kippington, living with his wife, Lillian Gilchrist Thompson. The couple had three sons, Piers, Austen, and Sidney and two daughters, Vera and Malys. Through the Thompson line they were cousins to the Rector of Sevenoaks, Reverend John Rooker and his wife, Adele nee Thompson. Archdeacon Dunkerley officiated at St John the Baptist church on St John's Hill, and Reverend Septimus Hebert ministered to his parish at nearby Seal.

St John's Church, where Archdeacon Dunkerley officiated

The Thompson and Rooker boys were educated locally. The 1901 census recorded Sidney Thompson as a pupil at the New Beacon Preparatory School, along with his distant cousins, Guy and (John) Kingsley Rooker. Their fellow pupils included the future war poet Siegfried Sassoon, and his younger brother, Hamo, who died in November 1915 in Turkey.

It was perhaps remarkable that from one small town, five sons of the local clergy were each awarded the Military Cross for various acts of gallantry during the war. The Bishop of Rochester certainly thought so, writing to the *Sevenoaks Chronicle* in 1918 to highlight '*an interesting fact*'.

All three of the serving Thompson brothers, who wore the King's uniform, took advantage of the opportunity afforded by the Essenhigh Corke photographic studio, where Henry Essenhigh Corke offered to photograph any serviceman or woman at no charge.

Despite his poor health and eyesight, Sidney Gilchrist Thompson obtained his Commission in August 1914 and was gazetted to the West Kent Yeomanry, in which he eventually became a temporary major. He was later appointed to the permanent rank of captain. He was sent to

Piers, Sidney, and Austen Thompson were photographed by
Henry Essenhigh Corke at his studio in the High Street

France in 1917 attached to the Royal West Kent Regiment and was awarded the Military Cross
(*London Gazette*, 16th September 1918).

The citation for Sydney's award read:

*For conspicuous gallantry and devotion to duty during an enemy attack. He command-
ed his Company most successfully, showing fine courage and sound judgement. He was
of great assistance to his commanding officer under very difficult circumstances, and
throughout set a high example to his men.*

Sidney Gilchrist Thompson

His brother, Austen, had passed through the Officer Training Corps when at school at Winchester College and was working as a clerk to a tea broker when he was commissioned to the

South Lancashire Regiment in October 1914. The following year he was sent, first to France and then on to Salonika, where he was awarded the Military Cross in June 1918 (the citation does not appear to have been published).

Austen Thompson wrote home to his parents in 1915 from the Front:

We have now been in these trenches since Friday, my Platoon is in small dug-outs along the road which goes past British Headquarters, the firing line is just over the ridge. I have got a dug-out which is fairly free from rats. The first night they ate all the food I had in my haversack, also my soap and my candles, the next night I had nothing for them to eat, and so they did not trouble me much. It is not pleasant to have them scrambling over you and dropping on to you from the roof during the night, but one can get used to anything.

Luckily it is still dry, but cold; we are in a hollow near some trees, so it will be damp later. The snipers are very troublesome – was wounded yesterday by one, but on the whole it is fairly quiet. I marvel at the way the men write to a selection of their relatives every day if they can get the paper, but I find it difficult to emulate them myself.

His brother, Piers, served with the 2/4th Battalion Royal West Kent Regiment and wrote to his parents on 13th January 1916, giving his address as '*A Tent on the Beach, Egypt*'.

Behold two sons of the Vicars of Sevenoaks in a tent together, listening to the sea roaring a few yards away, while the wind is whirling half the sands of Egypt against the tent walls. When I landed a terrible thing happened; my baggage suddenly vanished while I was collecting a few last things on the boat, and I was in despair that I would never see again the kit which we chose with such care and thought. However, after spending two days, and a fabulous sum in cab fares – I at last found it.

This place is a sort of Home for Lost Dogs; all men coming out of hospital, or from home, come here for a while before re-joining their units. I am 2nd in command of a Company, and the parades and the work are very much the same as in England.

Piers Thompson was taken prisoner at Gaza and was held until the end of the war, when he returned home suffering from malaria.

It was Cecil Dunkerley, son of Archdeacon Dunkerley of St John's, Sevenoaks, who took shelter with Piers Thompson in that tent in Egypt. He had been a member of the Cambridge University Officer Training Corps and served first as a lieutenant with 2/4th Royal West Kent Regiment and was later Captain with the Welch Divisional Staff. Cecil won the Military Cross and went on to serve as Deputy Assistant Provost Marshal in Egypt and entered Jerusalem with General Lord Allenby. His award appeared in the *London Gazette* on 16th August 1917, according to the citation:

For conspicuous gallantry and devotion to duty. After all the gun crews of a tank had become casualties he ascertained how to work the gun, and kept up fire during the withdrawal of the tank, thus preventing further counter-attacks on the part of the enemy. He displayed great gallantry and resource at a critical moment.

In July 1917, the *Sevenoaks Chronicle* reported that the Rector's son, Guy Rooker, of the Divisional Signal Company in the Indian Army Reserve, was said to have been involved in heavy fighting on the North West Frontier. A telegram later reached the Rectory informing his parents that he had been wounded but was recovering well in hospital.

The Rector's other, son, Kingsley, had been at the Front with 9th Machine Gun Corps before he was appointed Aide de Camp to General Kelly, who commanded 69th (2nd East Anglian) Division based at Thetford. He was subsequently Assistant Provost Marshal at Rouen. In autumn 1917 he was in England undertaking training in Lincolnshire. At the same time, his brother, Guy, now recovered from his injuries, was heading to Mesopotamia, having sent the previous three years in India.

Kingsley Rooker was awarded the Military Cross (*London Gazette*, 16th September 1918):

For conspicuous gallantry and devotion to duty during an evening attack. He displayed the utmost coolness under intense shell and machine gun fire, and gave the greatest confidence to his gun teams, and together with some infantry, held his position with great gallantry. He was finally wounded.

The Vicar of Seal, Reverend Hebert's son, Bernard Theodore Martyn Hebert, a lieutenant in the Welsh Guards, was awarded his Military Cross (*London Gazette*, April 1918):

For conspicuous gallantry and devotion to duty in remaining in charge of his platoon though wounded, superintending the relief, and taking out a wiring party and started them to work. He then returned to company headquarters in a fainting condition.

While all of the sons of the vicars of Sevenoaks were fortunate to survive the war, the Vicar of Kippington's nephew, Arnold Bosanquet Thompson, was killed in the Dardanelles on Christmas Day 1915. A memorial plaque was unveiled at St Mary, Kippington in September 1917.

Two of these clergymen's sons ultimately followed the example set by their fathers; Cecil Dunkerley, who had shown such bravery in that tank, was ordained and lived until 1978. His son, Flying Officer Michael Dunkerley was shot down and killed over France in November 1943.

Bernard Hebert was also ordained and lived until 1976 when he died in Wiltshire. His brother, Reverend Arthur Gabriel Hebert, had served as a chaplain with the YMCA during the war.

Austen Thompson emigrated to Canada, where he was killed in a motor accident in 1941. After the war his brother, Piers, was briefly a Member of Parliament for the Liberal party in the 1920s. He died in 1969. Sidney lived on until 1985, when he died in Tunbridge Wells.

Of the Rooker brothers, Kingsley had a distinguished career which included working with Duff Cooper as a counsellor at the British Embassy in Paris during the Second World War. He was at one point the British minister to the Gaullist National Committee. Kingsley Rooker was appointed to the Order of the British Empire in the Honours List of January 1945 in respect of his war work. He died in 1951. His brother, Guy, died in 1964 in Hampshire.

Daughters of the Clergy

The daughters of the local clergy also made significant contributions to the war effort. Malys Thomspon worked as an orderly at Cornwall Hall VAD hospital between 1916 and 1917. Her sister, Vera, nursed at the same hospital from September 1914 until May 1917. Her records show that she gave over 4,000 hours of nursing during those three years, after which she was loaned to the military hospital in Eastbourne.

Vera Thompson

Cecil Rooker, daughter of the Rector, also nursed at Cornwall Hall, having volunteered her services since 1912. A part time nurse, by December 1917 she had volunteered for over 5,000 hours. Cecil's sister, Margery, had been the Quartermaster of Cornwall Hall VAD from 1912 until 1913. She re-joined in 1917 as a trained nurse and assisted in the operating theatre. Rosemary Rooker also worked at Cornwall Hall from 1912, as Quartermaster and then as a nurse. She was also loaned to the hospital at Eastbourne from May 1917.

Archdeacon Dunklerley's daughter, Elfrida, had started to volunteer at St John's VAD in autumn 1913. She then volunteered again from October 1914 until June 1915. From November 1915 until March 1916 she nursed at the Federation of Malay States hospital (based in Hertfordshire) after which she trained to become an ambulance driver for the British Red Cross. Elfrida drove ambulances in England until January 1918, including working as a chauffeuse at Finborough Red Cross Hospital, Stowmarket, Suffolk. Keen to do more, from January 1918, Elfrida spent a year as an ambulance driver in France. She worked as part of the convoys at Etaples, Trouville and Boulogne. For her work she was awarded the British War Medal and the Victory Medal. Her sister, Mary Gwendoline, volunteered at St John's

VAD from February 1917. First employed in the kitchen, she was later working as a chauffeuse and was still volunteering in June 1919.

The Member of Parliament's Sons

By 1914, Henry William Forster had been the Member of Parliament for Sevenoaks for 22 years, holding the seat from 1892. A Deputy Lieutenant of Kent, he went on to serve as Financial Secretary to the War Office from 1915. Forster had married Rachel, daughter of the 1st Lord Montagu of Beaulieu, in 1890, and the couple had four children, John, Alfred Henry, Rachel and Emily.

Henry Forster later became MP for Bromley in 1918 and was ennobled in 1920 becoming 1st Baron Forster of Lepe in Southampton. From 1920 until 1925 he served as Governor General of Australia before returning home to England. He died in 1936 aged 69.

Forster's eldest son, John, was born on 13th May 1893 and was gazetted as Second Lieutenant Forster in the King's Royal Rifles on 3rd September 1913.

In the early days of the war the fact that the son of the local Member of Parliament was already at the Front was mentioned several times at public recruitment meetings in Sevenoaks, to demonstrate that the sons of the politicians and the gentry were already *'doing their bit'*.

John Forster was killed in the early hours of 14th September 1914 during the First Battle of the Aisne. His battalion had been ordered to advance to the plateau of Troyon and dig in. They went forward in bad weather and when they reached the crest, were unable to continue further and found themselves pinned down by enemy fire coming from the occupied sugar factory at the crossroads above Troyon.

John's death was reported in the *Sevenoaks Chronicle*, along with a letter that had been written to his parents:

> *I ought to have written before about your dear brave Jack, but I was shot through the head the same day and it has been impossible. He died like the gallant English gentleman that he was, leading his men at a critical time when men wanted leading. He was shot right through the head and never recovered. He was my best and brightest officer under all the most trying circumstances and his men all adored him – as of course we all did.*
>
> *The circumstances were as follows:*
>
> *Our Battalion was ordered out in advance of the Division to occupy some high ground and hold it while the Division passed. We were just getting up to the top at 4 a.m., when, at a point where the space between us and the top was almost perpendicular, we suddenly found ourselves being fired at in the dark by hundreds of Germans, who were firing right down on us as if we were in a rat-pit, so to speak. We had to force our way up to the top of the hill, and when we arrived there we found ourselves confronted by a strong force of Germans, entrenched with machine guns in position, and only 200 yards off. We remained there all day under a heavy shell and rifle fire.*
>
> *It was a terrible day for our Battalion. By mid-day there were only six Company officers left. We lost 15 officers out of 24 and 283 men. These heavy losses were mostly caused by those*

dirty Germans holding up their hands in token of surrender and then opening fire on us when we got within 20 yards of their trenches. I am so very sorry about your son. He was a first-class officer and a great favourite with his brother officers as well as his N.C.O's and men.

Lieutenant Alfred Henry Forster

John's brother, Alfred Henry, was born on 7th February, 1898 and educated at Winchester College before attending the Royal Military College, Sandhurst. He was commissioned in the 2nd Dragoons Guards (Royal Scots Greys) in July 1916.

Memorial to the Forster brothers at St Katherine's, Exbury

Alfred was sent to France the following February and was promoted to lieutenant on 19th January, 1918. On 17th October 1918 he was seriously wounded near Le Cateau and transferred to the Gerstley-Hoare Hospital for Officers at 53 Cadogan Square, Belgravia, London, where he spent five months before dying of his wounds on 10th March 1919.

While at the hospital, Alfred became friends with fellow patient, the sculptor Cecil Thomas. After Alfred's death, Lord and Lady Forster commissioned Thomas to design the remarkable memorial to John and his brother, which is in the church of St Katherine, at Exbury in the New Forest. The bronze figure was exhibited at the Royal Academy in 1924 and a model is held by the Victoria and Albert Museum.

The memorial, which displays a recumbent figure of Alfred, is inscribed:

To the Glory of God and in loving memory of their two sons John and Alfred who gave their lives for King and Country in the Great War 1914 -1918 this monument is erected by Lord and Lady Forster of Lepe.

There is a similar memorial in the church of All Hallows-by-the-Tower, London. It was Lord Forster's wish that this would not be a personal memorial but one to all those who had died. There are similar memorials at the church of St John, Southend and in Newcastle Cathedral, Australia.

There is also a memorial plaque to John Forster in the church at Exbury.

Memorial plaque to John Forster

The Forster family had previously lived at Southend Hall in Lewisham (now demolished) and Lord Forster donated the land for Forster Memorial Park near Catford in memory of his sons. The park was opened by his daughter, Dorothy, in 1922.

The brothers are also remembered at their schools and in the parliamentary books of remembrance at Westminster.

~

Part Eight

BURIED AT HOME

Buried at St Nicholas

The majority of men named on the Sevenoaks War Memorial are buried or remembered abroad in the immaculately maintained cemeteries and memorials of the Commonwealth War Graves Commission (CWGC). Some lie much closer to home, often because they were invalided back to England and were buried locally after dying of their wounds. There are CWGC graves at Greatness Cemetery and in local churches, in and around Sevenoaks. Many of these men were given a funeral with full military honours, which was reported in the *Sevenoaks Chronicle*.

At St Nicholas, the parish church of Sevenoaks, there are several memorials inside the church to some of the Sevenoaks fallen; others are interred in the churchyard or remembered on family graves despite being buried elsewhere.

Inside the church are memorials to John Sherbrooke Richardson, Geoffrey Harrison, George Henry Heslop, William Goss Hicks, and William Guy Cronk. Cronk is also mentioned on the tombstone on his parent's grave and was one of the earliest of the Sevenoaks casualties, being killed in 1914.

William Cronk is remembered on the
family grave in the churchyard

John Baldwin
1891 - 28th September 1915
Private 6634, 7th Reserve Cavalry Regiment (9th & 21st Lancers)

The funeral of John Baldwin, known as Jack, was held in the churchyard in 1915. He was the only man buried at St Nicholas to have died as a result of enemy action. He was the son of John, a carpenter and joiner, and his wife, Annie. The 1891 census shows John aged only two months living in Grove Road with his parents and siblings. The 1901 census shows Annie, now widowed, living with her daughter Rose and son-in-law, Edward, with her two younger children, Frank and Jack, at 8, Grove Road. By 1911 Jack, aged 20, is living with another sister, Alice, and her husband, William Morse, on the Gloucester Road, St Pancras. Jack Baldwin enlisted in Hertford and served with the Household Cavalry. He died on 28th September 1915.

The *Chronicle* carried a report of his funeral:

> *The deceased, who was formerly in the employment of Mr A. McAdam Laurie, was 24 years of age, and serving in the 9th Lancers, when he was fatally injured whilst engaged in trench digging. The cortege proceeded from Grove Road to the Parish church by a firing party with arms reversed and a detachment of deceased's regiment with lances reversed, the band discoursing the solemn strains of Chopin's Marche Funebre. The coffin, draped with a Union Jack, was drawn on a gun carriage…The scene at the graveside was most impressive and the customary three volleys were fired and the Last Post sounded.*

Herbert Alfred Sears
1882 - 26th October 1918
Private 3682, Labour Corps, Non Combatant Corps, Eastern Command Depot

The grave of Herbert Sears and his wife, Rose Agnes née Sivyer (1884-1918), who both died

The grave of Herbert Sears and his wife, Rose

within a week of each other during the influenza pandemic of late 1918, leaving five young children, is also in the churchyard. Herbert had run the Rectory Farm for the Rev John Rooker and, as a conscientious objector, had served with the Labour Corps.

Others remembered on family graves include Frederick Harold Bourne who fought with the Australian Imperial Force, and brothers Percy and Albert Hayward.

All of these men are remembered on the town War Memorial, while there are others who are buried in the churchyard but not named there.

Frank Powell
1874 - 3rd June 1916
Sergeant Major, Army Service Corps

Frank Powell is one of these men. His grave is marked by the traditional headstone of the Commonwealth War Graves Commission but, unusually, is surrounded by a family grave that names his wife, Edith Amy Blanche Bees (1882–1969) and daughter Winifred Frances Gwendoline Powell (1909–1984). Frank, a sergeant major in the Army Service Corps (67th Home Counties Division) died suddenly on Saturday 3rd June 1916. The *Sevenoaks Chronicle* recorded that:

Shortly after mid-day, the deceased walked up through the town and spoke to Mr Fulbrook about a game of billiards that was played the previous evening. He then appeared to be in his usual health and was in good spirits. Two or three minutes later however, he fell down in front of the side door of the Dorset Arms Hotel. A member of the R.A.M.C and several others rendered assistance but before medical aid could be summoned the unfortunate man had passed away.

Frank Powell's unusual grave in
St Nicholas churchyard

Deceased who was about thirty-eight years of age, was a popular non-commissioned officer, both among the corps and the townspeople to many of whom he had become known during his stay in Sevenoaks. A native of Gillingham, he had seen eighteen years' service in the army.

The funeral took place with full military honours …when the remains were interred in St Nicholas cemetery. The coffin, covered with the Union Jack, was conveyed to the church on a gun-carriage, supplied by a Home Counties Battery whilst the Middlesex Regiment provided a firing party and trumpeter who sounded the Last Post. The band of the Middlesex Regiment led the solemn procession which included a very large number of deceased's friends from the various units stationed in the town.

Frank appears to have been born in 1873 but lied when he enlisted in 1901, giving his age as 20, meaning that his grave shows his age as 36, rather than in his early forties.

Charles Nesfield Andrewes,
18th April 1876 - 29th November 1918
Lieutenant, Labour Corps

Charles was born in Horsham, Sussex, in 1876, the son of Nesfield Andrews (1844-1916) and his wife, Catherine nee Philips (1843-1919). He attended Trinity College, Cambridge and joined the South Devon Yeomanry in 1902. He served during the war as a lieutenant in the Labour Corps and died of influenza after the Armistice on 29th November 1918.

Bernard Paul Gascoigne Beanlands MC
9th September 1897 - 8th May 1919
Captain, Royal Flying Corps (formerly Hampshire Regiment)

Perhaps the most famous combatant in the churchyard is Captain Bernard Paul Gascoigne Beanlands, a Canadian flying ace credited with several victories.

Beanlands was born in Canada in September 1897 to Canon A.J. Beanlands (1857-1917) and his wife, Laura Maud née Hills (1859-1903), later of Wickhurst Manor, Sevenoaks Weald. He was educated at Oundle School before attending Sandhurst and joined the Hampshire Regiment in December 1914. Eventually serving as a lieutenant and spending seven months in the trenches, he was transferred to 70 Squadron of the Royal Flying Corp in May 1916 (achieving most of his kills with 24 Squadron). His first victory came in that September when he killed German aces Hans Rosencrantz and Wilhelm Fahlbusch. Later that year he was promoted to flight commander, serving as temporary captain. He scored eight more victories and was awarded the Military Cross (gazetted 25th April 1915) according to the citation:

'He has brought down three enemy aeroplanes out of control and driven down several others over the enemy lines'

The *Sevenoaks Chronicle* reported in 1917 that he had suffered gunshot wounds in both thighs, having been wounded once before. The paper noted:

Captain (Bernard) Paul Gascoigne Beanlands MC

He is at present at Brighton and has been out on parade on a spinal chair. It will be a long, slow cure. Captain Beanlands has the honour of being known as a very clever Airman and has been responsible for the fall of numerous enemy aircraft.

Paul Beanlands recovered, was later wounded again three days after his final victory in March 1918 and did not return to combat. He survived the war only to die in a flying accident at RAF Northolt on 8th May 1919. He was laid to rest next to his father in the churchyard at St Nicholas.

War Graves at Greatness Cemetery

The Commonwealth War Graves Commission estimates that there are 300,000 war graves and memorials in the UK and lists sixteen First World War graves at Greatness Cemetery.

Commonwealth War Graves at Greatness Cemetery

Only six of these men are remembered on the town War Memorial.

Some were evacuated home to Sevenoaks and died from their wounds. Others were taken ill unexpectedly or died accidentally, not having left the UK and were buried locally rather than returned to their home towns. Some had been patients at the local VAD hospitals. Three of the CWGC graves are of men who died after the end of the war. In addition, there are two private graves of soldiers who died after the official cut off for an official war grave in August 1921.

James Galligan
1881 - 4th November 1914
Sapper 6659, 1st Field Company, Royal Engineers

James Galligan was from St Helens, Lancashire, the son of Peter and Elizabeth. The 1911 census records him as a twenty-nine year old at home with his wife, Sarah Ann and two young sons: William aged four, and Peter, four months. James served with the No.1 Co West Lancashire Company of the Royal Engineers. He is recorded as dying of natural causes while lacing up his boots, at the Amherst Arms, Riverhead, (now a restaurant) near Sevenoaks. Galligan was the first soldier to be buried at Greatness Cemetery. His funeral was conducted with full military honours, his body conveyed to the cemetery on a gun carriage.

At a meeting of the Sevenoaks Urban Council, it was reported that only 35s was provided to bury a man. This was not enough to cover the cost of the coffin. The Council resolved to waive all of the burial costs and to write to the War Office, condemning the very poor provision made in such cases.

Harry McCarthy
1893 - 6th April 1915
Private 14889, 2nd Battalion, The Duke of Cornwall's Light Infantry

Harry McCarthy was born at Shinecroft Cottages in Otford, the third of nine children of John Richard McCarthy, a railway worker, and his wife, Sarah Ellen. Prior to the outbreak of war, he was listed as being a laundryman on the 1911 census. By that time the family was living in Moor Road, Sevenoaks.

The *Sevenoaks Chronicle* recorded Harry's funeral in some detail:

A most impressive spectacle was witnessed on Saturday at Greatness Cemetery, when, with full military honours the mortal remains of Pte H McCarthy, 2nd Duke of Cornwall's Light Infantry, were laid to rest in the site which has been set aside by the Sevenoaks Urban District Council for the burial of natives and former residents of Sevenoaks or inhabitants of the town who have taken part in the Naval and Military Expeditionary Forces of the Crown.

Deceased, who was only twenty-one years of age…enlisted, leaving a situation on the railway at Erith in September last. After some six months training he was drafted to the Front on 11th March and took part in the battle of Neuve Chapelle where he was wounded in the spine. McCarthy was taken to a hospital at Boulogne and then to Folkestone where he expired on Tuesday last.

Harry's coffin was covered with the Union Jack and borne from his home in Moor Road on a gun carriage by a team of six horses and preceded by the band of 5th Kings Own Royal Lancaster Regiment, which played the Dead March from Saul and Chopin's Funeral March.

According to the *Kent Messenger*:

The treble singers with Mr Neave and Mr Meeks of St John's Church Choir sang the hymn 'On the resurrection morning' at the graveside, after which a firing party from the 2/5th King's Own Royal Lancashire Regiment fired three volleys over the grave and the 'Last Post' was sounded.

Thomas Unsworth
1896 - 9th May 1915
Private 3916, 2/5th Battalion The Loyal North Lancashire Regiment

The *Sevenoaks Chronicle* reported details of the inquest into Private Unsworth's death on Friday 14th May 1915. According to John Bellows, a fellow soldier in the same regiment, the two men had decided to cycle to Oxted together. Bellows was riding behind Unsworth when he saw him fall as his bicycle slipped on the road, which, despite being fairly straight and flat, was greasy because of the soft tar. Private Unsworth was dragged about ten yards by the bike before two men of the Royal Army Medical Corps picked him up; they carried him to a nearby house where an ambulance was sent for and he returned to Sevenoaks.

Unsworth was admitted to the hospital at Cornwall Hall where he was examined by Dr Mansfield. In his testimony to the inquest the doctor stated that Unsworth was concussed and unconscious, having a bruise on his forehead and one on the back of his head. Private Unsworth never regained consciousness and died (from a haemorrhage caused by his fall) in the early hours of the following morning.

The funeral was held with full military honours and the coffin was conveyed to the Council offices by B Company of Private Unsworth's regiment, where it was transferred to a gun carriage and carried to the cemetery. Three volleys were fired and the Last Post sounded as he was laid to rest.

George Francis Fitzwalter Benest
1896 - 25th May 1915
Private 2877, 2/4th Battalion King's Own (Royal Lancaster Regiment)

George Benest was born in Bebbington, Cheshire, in 1896. He was the son of George and his wife, Gwitha. He enlisted at Ulverston, most likely in August 1914, and was based in Sevenoaks with his regiment when he died at Tonbridge Hospital. He is remembered on the War Memorial at Broughton-in-Furness.

Ernest Edward Mitchell
2nd April 1886 - 13th March 1916
Leading Stoker, K/13729, HMTB 11, Royal Navy

Ernest Mitchell was born and grew up in Beckenham, the son of William, a bricklayer and his wife, Laura. Ernest married Lilian Charlotte Tolhurst on 11th November 1908 at Wandsworth and the couple went on to have four children, Ernest, Dorothy Ellen, William Louis, and Alfred James.

His records show that he was working as a printer's machine minder when he joined the Royal Navy on 2nd April 1909. He served first on the *Nelson* and then the *Jupiter* and the *Prince of Wales* before becoming a stoker on 24th January 1912. Ernest was serving on HM Torpedo Boat 11 and on patrol in the North Sea when it was struck by a German mine with the loss of all 24 crew members.

Ernest Alfred Bence
1878 - 29th April 1916
Regimental Serjeant Major, L4803 2/9th Battalion Middlesex Regiment

Ernest Bence was born in 1878 in Islington, the son of Frederick, a compositor and printer, and his wife, Emma. The 1911 census shows that Bence was with the 2nd Battalion of the Middlesex Regiment. He was with 2/9th Middlesex Regiment stationed in Sevenoaks when he was found dead by his colleague, Company Sergeant Major Henry Charles Thorn, on 29th April 1916, having apparently shot himself with his revolver. According to newspaper reports, Thorn had gone to see if Serjeant Bence was coming for his dinner at around 14.30. No-one had heard a shot being fired but he testified that his fellow sergeants had been in the mess and there was generally a lot of noise. The inquiry heard how Bence had recently been arrested for a disciplinary offence but nothing had yet been proved; his conduct was

SOLDIER'S TRAGIC DEATH

INQUEST ON TUESDAY.

Coroner Buss held an enquiry on Tuesday afternoon at the Sevenoaks Urban Council's Offices touching the death of Regimental Sergt.-Major Ernest Alfred Bence, who met with a tragic death on Saturday last at Sevenoaks. Mr. W. Edwards was elected foreman of the jury.

Annie Maud Wywne Bence, widow of deceased, said she resided at the Drill Hall, Staines. She thought deceased was about 39. He was a regimental sergt.-major in the 2/9th Middlesex. She saw him about a fortnight ago at Staines. He had good health generally, and when she last saw him he was in his usual health. He had no trouble of any kind to her knowledge. He was of a very happy and bright disposition. He had something the matter with his teeth a little while ago but nothing more. She was communicated with respecting his death and she came to Sevenoaks and identified the body.

The *Sevenoaks Chronicle* carried a detailed report of the Inquest

generally good and if he had been found guilty, the punishment would have been light, not more than a demotion to sergeant.

Lieutenant Quarter Master W R Shepherd had known Serjeant Bence well and gave evidence to the inquest that Bence had been practicing cleaning his revolver recently, and some cleaning materials were found on the scene. His body had been discovered lying on his back with his head underneath the bed and a bullet wound to his left breast. His revolver was lying on a table with its butt toward the bed and had been issued to him at the end of March as part of his kit. According to the newspaper:

> *It seemed from the position of the chair and the body that the deceased had been 'fiddling' or 'playing' with the revolver. It was not customary to have it loaded but the deceased had only been issued with ammunition recently...Before deceased was a Company Serjeant he was a Colour-Sergeant and they did not carry revolvers. Deceased was a thorough man and a good soldier, but he did not think he would understand a revolver.*

Second Lieutenant Bryan reported that within the last 10 days he had been together with the deceased practicing revolver shooting when, after firing off several rounds, Serjeant Bence had reloaded his revolver when it had suddenly gone off and hit the ground yards away *'the pull-off being very light'*.

Serjeant Bence's widow, Annie Maud Wywne Bence, who resided at the Drill Hall at Staines, stated that she had last seen her husband when he had visited Staines a fortnight before his death when he had appeared in his usual health, with nothing appearing to trouble him, his usual disposition being *'happy and bright'*.

Dr Brown who examined the body stated that the deceased had died from syncope as a result of internal bleeding, having shot himself, at the table at very close range.

An open verdict was recorded and Serjeant Bence was buried with full military honours at Greatness Cemetery.

George Bernard Taylor
1889 - 26th July 1916
Private G/12547, 7th Battalion, The Queen's Own Royal West Kent Regiment

George Taylor was the son of William, a house painter and his wife, Mary, of 4, Cobden Road.

In the 1911 census, George working as a gardener, while a few years later his service papers show that he was working as a plumber when he joined up in early 1916. He was confined to barracks for five days for *'Improper conduct on the line of march'*, while stationed at Fort Darland in Kent. He arrived in France that June, joining his Battalion on 6th July.

On 13th July George received a gunshot wound to his left leg, resulting in fracture and gangrene. He was evacuated from France to the 1st Birmingham War Hospital, where he died as a result of his wounds on 26th of July 1916. He was buried at Greatness Cemetery and the *Kent Messenger* carried an account of the funeral in its edition on 5th August. The 2/7th Devon Regiment provided a firing party and funeral bearers.

George Taylor's grave on the hundredth
anniversary of his death

George Taylor is the only man buried in Greatness to have died from wounds sustained during the Battle of the Somme.

Henry Ramsdale
1875 - 17th October 1916
Private G/13035, 3rd Battalion, Royal Sussex Regiment

Henry Ramsdale was born in Sevenoaks to Silas, a coal seller of Cobden Road and his wife, Sarah. By 1891 the family had moved to Bethel Road and Henry was working at the local laundry. He married Clara Jane Pickering in 1900. The 1901 census shows the couple living on Golding Road and both working in the laundry. Ten years later and the couple are living with their five daughters on Sandy Lane.

Henry joined the Royal Sussex Regiment when he was called up. His service records have not survived but the *Kent Messenger* reported that, having joined the army in June 1916, he was sent to France in September and was taken ill while crossing, being sent to hospital in Calais on arrival. He stayed for four days before being sent to hospital in Birmingham but was discharged and returned home, dying shortly after. The paper recorded that he had never been a strong man and there had been surprise when he was passed fit for active service.

Herbert Thomas Lloyd
1892 - 30th January 1917
Private 2439, Dorset Yeomanry (Queen's Own)

Herbert Lloyd was born in Westerham, to George and Elizabeth. The *Sevenoaks Chronicle* reported in its 2nd February edition that Private Lloyd was a shoeing-smith who had recently transferred from the West Kent Yeomanry to the Dorset Regiment. He had died of a cerebral haemorrhage. A military funeral was held and three volleys fired over his grave.

Edward Stigant Carruthers
1866 - 16th May 1917
Major, Royal Engineers

Edward Carruthers was born in Chatham in 1866. An Inspector of Works with the Royal Engineers, he had returned to Sevenoaks in May 1917 to attend the funeral of his late father, who had died aged 86. The funeral was held in Chatham and, after returning to Sevenoaks, Major Carruthers was taken ill and died suddenly that evening at his home, *The Laurels*, on St John's Road. The funeral was held on the Saturday when, according to the *Chronicle*, large bodies of men from the Essex Yeomanry and the Hertfordshire Yeomanry followed the cortege to Greatness Cemetery, preceded by a firing party, and the band playing Handel's Dead March.

Frederick George Dobson
1874 - 7th July 1917
Private 13169, Royal Army Service Corps

Frederick Dobson appears to have been born in Margate in 1874. His army pension records show that he was working as a hotel porter when he first enlisted with the army in 1895 aged 20, going on to serve as a gunner with the Royal Artillery. He served in India and had a good service record until he was invalided out of the army in 1901 on health grounds. He re-enlisted in 1915 when he was nearly 41, was sent to France and served with the Army Service Corps.

Frederick reported sick in 1916 and was diagnosed with a gastric ulcer and discharged as unfit for further active or home service. He died the following year, aged 43 and is buried in Greatness cemetery.

Arthur Sidney Piper
1876 - 28th August 1919
Sergeant 200044, 1/5th Battalion The Queen's Own Royal West Kent Regiment

Arthur Piper was born in Hildenborough, the son of John and Charlotte. Arthur served as a Territorial from 1908 and had been employed as a railway guard for several years. During the war he served in India from March 1917 until January 1919.

SHOREHAM FATALITY.

FUNERAL OF MR. A. S. PIPER.

The funeral of Mr. A. S. Piper, whose tragic death at Shoreham whilst engaged on his duties as guard on the S.E. and C. Railway reported in our last issue, took place at Greatness Cemetery on Friday. The service was conducted by the Ven. Archdeacon Dunkerley. The coffin was borne to its last resting place by the companions of the deceased in the S.E. and C.R. services, a large contingent of whom, under Mr. Thomas, Stationmaster at Tubs Hill Station, attended the funeral and preceded the cortege.

The principal mourners were: Mrs. Piper (widow), Miss Nellie Piper (daughter), Mr. Piper (father), Mrs. Searle (sister), Mr. Jupp (brother-in-law), Messrs. Arthur and Albert Jupp (brother-in-law), Mrs. A. Jupp, Mr. D. Sears, Mr. Edwyn Smith, Mr. Driver and Miss Renolds. Col. C. J. Laurie, deceased's Commanding Officer in the old Territorials, was also present.

Wreaths and floral tributes were received from his heartbroken wife and children; From Dad Neil and Dave; From Annie and Arthur; From Mum, Dad and family; From Dave and Betty; Rose and Ted; Mrs. Brooks and family and the neighbours of Chatham Hill; Members of the Sevenoaks Branch N.U.R. A beautiful artificial wreath was also sent from the staffs at Tubs Hill and Bat and Ball Stations.

Mr. W Hodges had charge of the arrangements.

Mrs. Piper and family wish to thank all kind friends for the expressions of sympathy, and also for floral tokens.

How the *Sevenoaks Chronicle*
reported Arthur's funeral

Described in his obituary as a popular NCO, he was demobilised only months before his death. Arthur was killed in an accident during the routine shunting of trains at Shoreham station. The inquest reached a verdict of accidental death but how it was caused remained unknown.

John Thomas Fisher
1881 - 17th October 1918
Gunner 83338, Royal Garrison Artillery

John Fisher was born in Spitalfields, the son of John and Annie. He was married with three children and working as a clerk when he joined up in May 1916. During the war, John served at home with the Anti Aircraft Artillery. He had been a patient at the Cornwall Hall Hospital with pneumonia since September 1917. Gunner Fisher had lived at Clerkenwell, London and was survived by his wife and family.

Reginald Frederick Sudds
1896 - 16th December 1919
Lance Corporal 204838, 1st Battalion, Devonshire Regiment

Reginald Sudds was the third son of Edward, a coachman and his wife, Annie, who lived at 46, Cobden Road. By the time he was 15, Reginald was working as a bottle washer in a local brewery.

Reginald appears to have enlisted in 1915, first with the Royal West Kent Regiment and later serving with the Royal Devonshire Regiment, where he reached the rank of lance corporal. He served in the Dardanelles as part of the Gallipoli campaign, and then in Egypt. He died in December 1919 not of wounds but of an unspecified disease contracted while abroad, and was buried in Greatness Cemetery.

William Fuller
1888 - 5th July 1920
Private L/14263, 1st Battalion The Queen's Own Royal West Kent Regiment

William Fuller was the son of John Fuller a foreman platelayer, and his wife, Jane. In 1891 the family were living at 7, Old Greatness, Sevenoaks. By 1901 the Fuller family was living at 1, Greatness Road. It is possible that William, who is not living at that address is the William Fuller listed as 'under detention' at the Kent County Industrial School at Kingsnorth, Ashford. When he enlisted in September 1906, William stated that he had been apprenticed as a tailor. His records show that he was 18 years and 9 months, being just over 5'4" tall with grey eyes and brown hair. The 1911 census shows that he was serving with 1st Battalion of the Royal West Kent Regiment.

His military papers note that his conduct was indifferent, while also recording that he was hardworking. Numerous drunken incidents, absences and theft, appear on his conduct sheet throughout his years of service.

William was sent to France with the Expeditionary Force on 13th August 1914. At about the same time his wife, Harriet, was admitted to the Sevenoaks workhouse, suffering from partial paralysis, having given birth five weeks previously. The Soldiers' Sailors' Families Association (still supporting veterans in Sevenoaks today) attempted to intervene on her behalf, as the separation allowance which she was entitled to was not being paid while she was 'in a state institution'.

William returned home after 46 days, on 29th September and did not return to the Front until two years later in September 1916, where he remained until January 1919. After the war, he sought to reenlist and, despite his previous conduct, it was noted on his application that he was:

A very smart and intelligent man; has previously served 13 years Colour Service and wishes to reenlist to complete 21 years service in order to qualify for a pension.

He was stationed at Maidstone and died at the Fort Pitt Military Hospital in Chatham of pneumonia. A private rather than a military funeral was held, in accordance with his family's wishes.

George Thomas Slade
1892 – 26th August 1920
Corporal 9656, 1/4th Battalion The Queen's Own Royal West Kent Regiment

George Thomas Slade was born in Sevenoaks in 1892. He was the son of William, a labourer, and his wife, Annie, who lived at 1, Hartslands Road. George's brother, John (1890-1916) had served with 6th Battalion Royal West Kent Regiment and died of his wounds in March 1916 (and is remembered on the Sevenoaks War Memorial). His brother, Charley, served with 3rd then 7th Battalions of the Royal West Kent Regiment and lost a leg during the war. John and George had followed in the footsteps of elder brother, William, who enlisted in 1900, saw action in South Africa and then served with The Buffs (East Kent Regiment), during the First World War.

George was a Territorial in G Company 1/4th Royal West Kent regiment from 1909 until 1911 when he joined the regular army in the August 1911. He was posted to India in October 1912, where he remained for most of the war.

George was severely wounded by a gunshot wound to his left jaw. In March 1919 he was transferred to Reserve, Section 'B' and demobilized. He was awarded a pension of 12s a week and regarded as having 40% disability caused by the gunshot wound to face and chest. He died on 26th August 1920, at 4 Kemp Cottages, Sevenoaks.

The grave of George Slade, who died
of his wounds in August 1920

Arthur Chapman
1874 – 1921
Pioneer 116131, Royal Engineers

There are two other graves which, although private family plots, lie with the men officially commemorated. One of these is the grave of Arthur Chapman who died on 11th October 1921, aged 47. Arthur, who had spent six years in the West Kent Militia, was 41 and living at 76, Bethel Road, when he joined up on 19th August 1915. He had been working for the Callender Cable Company and served as a pioneer in the Royal Engineers. He was discharged in July 1917 as being no longer fit for active service and was entitled to wear the Silver War Badge. This was awarded to those who had been honourably discharged owing to wounds or sickness. The badge was worn on their civilian clothes to show that they had previously served.

Arthur Chapman died shortly after the end of the qualifying period for an official Commonwealth War Grave

John Henry Simmons
1883 - 25th September 1921
Private 61939, 23rd Battalion, Royal Fusiliers

The 1911 census shows John Henry Simmons living at 5, St John's Place, with his wife, Alice, their two children, and John's mother and sister. John was employed as a scaffolder. He enlisted on 12th December 1915, most likely under the Derby Scheme. His service records have

Like Arthur Chapman, John Simmons was
buried among the official war graves. His
rank was recorded on his headstone

not survived but it appears that he first served with 12th Battalion East Surrey Regiment from
October to November 1916 before transferring to the Royal Fusiliers. He was discharged on
30th March 1918 as a result of his wounds and was entitled to wear the Silver War Badge.

St Mary's Church, Riverhead

There are two further war graves close to Sevenoaks at the churchyard of St Mary's, Riverhead.

Arthur Shingleton
30th December 1896 – 12th February 1915
Driver 1624, Royal Field Artillery

Arthur Shingleton, was born in Dover to Thomas and his wife, Ellen Elizabeth. He was ed-
ucated at Trinity School, Dover, and joined the Royal Field Artillery on 30th October 1914.
He died as a result of a brain haemorrhage after being struck by a runaway horse on 12th
February 1915, aged 18.

Aurea Lambarde

Bridget Aurea Teresa Lambarde
1889 – 5th March 1919

Bridget (known as Aurea) Lambarde had been Commandant at St John's VAD Hospital from October 1914 until July 1915. A member of the prominent Lambarde family of Bradbourne Hall, she died of heart failure following influenza, aged 29, on 5th March 1919, while working at the Royal Naval Hospital, Portland, Dorset.

~

Part Nine

ARMISTICE & AFTER

Armistice

News of the abdication of the Kaiser was brought to the town by a message to the offices of the *Kent Messenger* on the evening of Saturday 9th November at around 17.30. On the morning of Monday 11th, rumour abounded and the crowds of local people waited for news of the expected ceasefire. At 11.13 news of the Armistice was received at the *Kent Messenger* and a notice placed in their window. Quickly flags began to appear all over the town, heralding the arrival of peace. The parish church flew the Cross of St George and the Royal Ensign. Flags and bunting quickly appeared in the shops and were:

> *Eagerly bought by an overjoyed populace, so that motor cars, motor buses, ambulances, cars, baby carriages were quickly bedecked. Children were also carrying flags, and even sober-sided ladies of mature age were seen with small flags stuck in their handbags.*
>
> *The wounded soldiers from the hospitals were soon in the forefront of events. They formed a procession, headed with a band. Their instruments were not orthodox, and were not quite up to military pattern (in fact the cymbals looked suspiciously like a pair of dustbin covers), but they served the purpose. Other Tommies were driven through the town in motor cars, blowing trumpets, ringing bells, and singing for all they were worth. As soon as the bellringers could be got together a merry peal was rung on the parish church bells.*

When news of the Armistice was received, a small crowd gathered at the Fountain at the top of the High Street, where prayers had been said for the men at the Front on a daily basis. Many townspeople attended evensong and special thanksgiving services.

The celebrations continued all week. Fireworks could be heard throughout the town and some wounded soldiers paraded an effigy of the Kaiser in a barrow before setting fire to the figure on a bonfire.

With the lighting of some street lamps in the evening, it felt literally as if the town was emerging from the darkness of the long years of war.

A large thanksgiving service was held in the Market Place on the Wednesday afternoon. By three o'clock the crowd stretched as far as the eye could see as school children, nurses, the wounded, all attended, standing with those who had lost loved ones during their conflict. There were other soldiers in the crowd too.

In his address, the Rector, the Reverend Rooker:

Emphasised God's wondrous, immeasurable mercies to the people of the British Empire. …He spoke tenderly of those who had laid down their lives, urging all present to try to be worthy of the great sacrifices made for them. It was a notable fact that the British Empire under God had saved the world. As an Empire we had never stood higher. … All classes, rich and poor, had stood firmly and loyally during the terrible days of war.

The service ended with the National Anthem and then three cheers for the King and Queen, three more for the men of the armed forces, and a final three for the wounded soldiers amongst the crowd.

Crowds gathered in the Market Place to celebrate news of the Armistice and hear the Rector and other churchmen preach

The Rector later recalled the scene in his memoir:

> *…the most wonderful sight was in the Market Place on Wednesday afternoon, November 13th. There was a huge crowd of over 2000 people gathered together. The boys and girls of the Lady Boswell school, with the Infant School were close up to the harmonium. The clergy stood in a cart. I wish you all could have seen the sight from that cart, for it was the most splendid sight I ever saw in Sevenoaks. We sang our hymns and gave God thanks for the victory; and I tried to tell the people what it meant for us. And then we remembered the men of Sevenoaks who had given their lives for England. We were all silent for a few minutes, and then we said 'Our Father' under the open sky. And once again we sang 'God Save the King.'*

A Thanksgiving Service was held at St Nicholas' that Sunday. Again the Rector later recalled:

> *What a crowd there was! How glad we all were! How heartily we sang! But perhaps what most will remember is something that happened just before the service began.*
>
> *The Choir and Clergy came up through the West doors, and at the end of the procession came two officers holding a flag between them. One officer was Commander McKinnon, of the battleship 'The Barham' who had fought in the battle of Jutland; and the other was Major Ross, commanding the Scots Guards then in Sevenoaks, He had fought in the battle of Mons, 1914. They came up to the chancel, and reverently laid the flag, a Union Jack, on the Holy Table, and I said a prayer, asking God to give us thankful hearts (as we laid this flag of our Empire on his altar) and acknowledging that He had given us, and He alone, the victory.*
>
> *The flag hangs on the south side of the altar, and there is another flag opposite to it. It is one of the flags that flew from the British battle cruiser 'Indomitable' when the German fleet came in to surrender after the Armistice was signed.*

Gradually life began to return to normal. Men started to return home, although there were still sorrows; five of the men remembered on the town's War Memorial died after the Armistice, some of natural causes such as pneumonia, and others of their wounds. By early February 1919, the VAD hospitals were closing and other vestiges of the war, such as the YMCA hut on the Vine, which had seen many soldiers take advantage of its welcome during the war years, was shut. The National Kitchen was closed in the March as was the Hospital Supply Depot. Perhaps more controversially, the football goalposts were removed from the Vine. 'Three Demobilised Soldiers' wrote to the *Chronicle* on the matter asking:

> *Do the members of the Council realise that the 'unemployed youths' are soldiers who have been demobilised and are enjoying their 28 days furlough?*

Men returned from the Front began to resume their former lives. The *Chronicle* announced that G. Ellis of St John's had resumed business as a hairdresser; Sidney Blackman of the Royal West Kent Regiment was demobilised after four years' service and opened his premises as a tailor on Bank Street. Mr E Fielder, who had served with 1st Battalion Royal West Kent

A Victory Arch was erected to welcome
returning servicemen home

Regiment, resumed his business as a photographer and picture frame maker at Belgrave Terrace, Lower St John's.

The re-formation of the town band was welcomed by many, as was the return of cricket. A meeting was held in the Rose and Crown Hotel to re-establish football matches in the town and a series of games were arranged for the ground on Hollybush Lane in April 1919.

A meeting was held to establish a local club for ex-servicemen. Lord Sackville attended the initial meeting at which it was proposed to use the Drill Hall as the venue for the club. The Club would be open to former servicemen from the town and surrounding villages. The plans were the subject of an editorial in the *Chronicle*, which noted:

> *Now that 'the boys' were coming home in increasing numbers, the new Club will fill a want which the experiences of Army life has produced, somewhere where all can meet on the same level and find recreation for body and mind. Here also cooperation among the members will strengthen their hand in seeing that the town for which they endured untold hardships is made a better, happier and more progressive town than it may have been in the past.*

A similar meeting, that of the Sevenoaks branch of the Comrades of the Great War, was held at the Oddfellows Club. While stressing that the organisation was a democratic one, open to all former comrades, regardless of rank or class, some discordant notes were struck by Colonel

Ashley MP, Chairman of the national organisation. Ashley spoke of the issue of unemployment amongst former servicemen, along with the particular difficulties facing the disabled men.

'Women', he said, '*had done excellent work during the war, but the time had come when they should be genuinely thanked for their services and asked to go back to what they were doing before the war, and their jobs be given to discharged men*'.

These themes of equality between men, of the post war world of 1919 being different from that of 1914, and yet the need for women to return to their former ways of life, were repeated in meetings, services and newspaper editorials. Mrs Mackinnon, who spoke at the thanksgiving service in the Market Square was clear on this: the women of Sevenoaks would rise to their duties.

> *What were these duties? They were to make England a purer, better and brighter land, and it could be done by the women of England making happier homes. She concluded by appealing to the women of Sevenoaks to try and make their homes purer and happier, more unselfish, thinking more of others than themselves. If they undertook that duty then England would be a happier and better land.*

Although an increasing number of former servicemen were returning home, many were still overseas. One letter published in the *Sevenoaks Chronicle* from a 'Tunbridge Wellian' no doubt struck a chord with many Sevenoaks residents when he wrote from India complaining that like many of his comrades he had joined up for 'hostilities only' when he had enlisted at a recruitment meeting in 1914:

> *Now, my comrades and myself find ourselves here, in India, with no hopes of coming home. I wonder what that Committee, who promised so many good things is doing to help the local 1914-15 lads in India to get their release. If the same Committee will do as much shouting to get us home as they did in 1914 to get us to join up they would win the gratitude of all the Wells boys in India.*

This correspondence prompted a reply from Earl Stanhope, that not everyone had forgotten the 4th Royal West Kent Regiment in India. Stanhope had recently secured the passing of an amendment in the House of Lords to exclude men who had been serving in the Territorial Force before 4th August 1914 from further service in the Army after peace was signed. Although the Commons refused to accept the amendment, Stanhope assured that '*we have every intention of pressing the Government to bring it (the regiment) home at the earliest moment, consistent with a proper care for the health of those who have served their country so well*'.

News of the signing of the Treaty of Versailles – Peace! - was received in Sevenoaks via the offices of the *Chronicle* on 28th June 1919 and a brief statement was placed in the newspaper's window: *Peace signed at 3.12 pm today*.

Within 45 minutes, a pre-arranged signal of two long blasts from the siren at the Sevenoaks waterworks sounded. Soon residents and businesses began bedecking the High Street and London Road with flags.

Crowds began to flock into the town and the town band paraded through the streets, stopping at the Fountain to play Land of Hope and Glory, with a firework display commencing as they approached. Good natured crowds stayed in the streets until later that evening and many returned the following day for a religious service held in the Market Square, led by the Rector but including all denominations. A later service was held that afternoon on The Vine and similar services of thanksgiving held in every local place of worship. Congregations gathered not only to give thanks but to remember those of their former townsmen who had not returned.

In its editorial of the following issue, the *Sevenoaks Chronicle* observed:

> *Never since 1914 has Sevenoaks witnessed such an influx of visitors as on Monday last. Tempted, no doubt, partly by the general holiday spirit which seems to have impregnated people of all classes throughout the country and partly by the glorious weather conditions which prevailed, visitors flocked into and through the town from early morn until the day was well spent. They came by train and brake, by bicycle and by every sort of conveyance that could be extemporised for the purpose of transit, and they swept through the town to places further afield in all kinds of motors, from the elegant Rolls-Royce to ancient patterns of carts that one would have thought long ago were relegated to the limbo of things forgotten. Tradesmen's delivery vans equipped with temporary seats, motor cycles with and without sidecars, and the more humble push bike were also there, the whole forming a medley of traffic, streamed along the highways in an almost unbroken procession – going and coming – until the shades of night had fallen. Among those who made Sevenoaks the centre of the day's enjoyment, a large proportion spent the greater of their time amidst the beauties of Knole, whose wide acres and tree-clad slopes gave wide scope for health-giving enjoyment.*

Despite the sense of relief and celebration which swept the town, the formal celebrations of peace were a bitter disappointment. In a caustic review the *Chronicle* lambasted the official events:

> *Where, for the most part, the impressions have been one of bitter disappointment and resentment at the callous indifference of those, or most of those, who, acting on authority and without consulting the wishes of the people, followed their own inclinations and allowed the greatest day in our grand old country's history to pass practically unhonoured and unrecognised.*

So feeble was the effort that the paper felt justified in labelling the efforts in Sevenoaks a laughing stock in comparison to those of the surrounding villages, where many residents fled to instead, with others heading further to Tunbridge Wells to join in the celebrations there.

The children's sports and tea for approximately 1,100 of the town's youngest residents was seen as the one bright spot in the day. A 'comic' cricket match on the Vine was viewed with bemusement. While an evening concert at the YMCA was seen as a success, many felt that they had been let down by the inadequate organisation

Some local residents took matters into their own hands and on the Monday evening a large crowd gathered in Beech Road to watch the fireworks organised there with a huge bonfire and much community spirit in evidence. Residents of Hartslands Road, organised by Mrs Miles of the Stoneville Laundry, led a parade of about 40 children in costume through the town returning to her home for tea and later a bonfire and fireworks in her garden.

There was a sense that the official celebrations had been imposed on local people, who had not been consulted, with the organising committee apparently frowning on the idea of a carnival. The *Chronicle*, a champion of those who had served, was clear in its view:

> *There are in this town somewhere about 700 men who have been 'over there'. Men who faced danger and death for the sake of their loved ones. Ask these men what opportunities they have had during the past five years of such enjoyment as a carnival would have provided. Life in the trenches, with its nerve-destroying tension was not exactly 'one long song'. Now these boys are home, and on a day like Saturday last, surely something could have been done for them beyond a 'comic cricket match' and a concert? We have more faith in these men than to believe their thoughts would be altogether driven from the memory of their chums who lie 'out yonder'.*

More positive news came when some Sevenoaks residents closely associated with the war effort were recognised. Elizabeth Findlay was honoured with the award of an OBE. From 1902 until 1916 she had been assistant matron and superintendent of the YWCA Home of Rest in Sevenoaks, only relinquishing her role in July 1916 to become superintendent of the YWCA munitions hut at Crayford. Hon. Violet Mills, daughter of Lord Hillingdon, was awarded the OBE for her work at the VAD hospital at Wildernesse. Mrs Skilbeck, the commandant of Chevening VAD hospital since 1916 was appointed MBE.

THE HON. VIOLET MILLS, M.B.E.
SEAL V.A.D., KENT 5.
The Seal Detachment, the third women's detachment of the V.A.D. to be raised in Kent, was started by the Hon. Violet Mills in 1910, and came into active service after war was declared, when a Hospital was equipped at Wildernesse by the kindness of Lord Hillingdon with accommodation for 24 patients in two wards and a fully-equipped operating theatre with X-ray apparatus. Later a supplementary ward, with nine beds, was added.
The Hon. Violet Mills holds the five years' service badge from the British Red Cross and the "blue stripe" for qualifying in nursing.

Hon. Violet Mills was awarded the OBE for the running of Wildernesse Hospital

Lieutenant De Barri Crawshay

De Barri Crawshay of *Rosefield*, Sevenoaks, who had performed many useful roles during the war, notably as transport officer for the ten VAD hospitals in the Sevenoaks area was also honoured.

Major John Sterry, Assistant County Director for the Sevenoaks VAD Division, was awarded the OBE. He had had a long involvement with the local VAD and, together with Vita Sackville West, had established the VAD Kent 56. During 1916 to 1917 he had served with the RAMC in the Persian Gulf and Egypt, later returning home and serving as medical officer at St John's Hospital.

War Memorials

Much effort was turned to the question of war memorials and the discussion, planning, and eventual unveiling was regularly reported in the local press. Memorial plaques to some individuals were placed in churches and other places. Some had been erected during the course of the war and others were now added, with memorials to individual servicemen at St Nicholas, St Mary, Kippington, St John's Congregational Church, and The Drive Methodist Church. Other memorials, including one to the former staff of the Post Office who had fallen, along with the Roll of Honour of their colleagues who returned home, were also unveiled. The Post Office memorial was originally placed in the Sorting Office, and Lord Sackville spoke to mark the occasion. Eighty-nine men who worked for the postal service in the Sevenoaks district had enlisted and fourteen had not returned. The memorial is still on display but is now outside the modern Post Office building in South Park.

The site for the main Sevenoaks War Memorial was eventually agreed and commissioned for ground formerly known as the 'wasteland' opposite The Vine. The Memorial was funded by public subscription, including from house-to-house collections, with individual donations of up to £500. The total raised being £5,663.

THE VINE, SEVENOAKS.

After much discussion, the land opposite The Vine was donated by
Lord Sackville and was agreed as an appropriate site for the war memorial

It was unveiled on an autumn Sunday in October 1920 when hundreds of local people
assembled on The Vine to pay their public tribute to the memory of 225 sons of Sevenoaks,
who lost their lives during the conflict. The *Sevenoaks Chronicle* subsequently noted in its report of the event how every class was represented and had suffered loss, all had been bound
together in one great act of sacrifice.

On the afternoon of the unveiling the memorial was covered with the Union Jack, with
the town's coat of arms. Lord Sackville and the Bishop of Rochester led proceedings and
were joined by many other official representatives. The relatives of the men stood in their
own enclosure and a boy scout stood at each corner of the mound. Nurses and staff from the
local VAD hospitals attended, as did many of the local churches and other organisations, all
gathered to honour their fellow townsmen. The choirs of St Nicholas, St Mary, Kippington,
and St John's led the singing and the ex-servicemen marched to their places from nearby St
John's Congregational Church. The reformed town band accompanied the service.

After hymns had been sung and prayers said, Lord Sackville, who had served throughout
the war himself, spoke movingly:

*I suppose there can be no occasion which calls for greater unity of feeling than an oc-
casion like the present, when we meet here together for the purpose of unveiling and
dedicating a Memorial to our fellow towns-men who fought and died in the Great War.
It was inevitable that there should be divergence of opinion as to the particular form
that any Memorial should take; it is inevitable that there should be criticism of the site
chosen and of a dozen other matters: but I think that I may safely say that this gathering, as fully representative of all the various interests in this town of Sevenoaks, is united*

here today with one common thought, to pay tribute to the memory of those whose names you will find inscribed on this Memorial.

Many of these men were known to many of us: some of them met their end in my own regiment with me, and they went forth from Sevenoaks, hoping no doubt, that they might be safely spared to return in all safety, knowing full well the dangers they were going to encounter and yet facing those dangers with that cheerful uncomplaining acquiescence for the call of duty which has won for them a place in our esteem which no Memorial can ever adequately fill... I am glad to know that there are many in the assembly today of the men who were the comrades in arms of those whose memory we are honouring today.

He concluded by speaking of the relatives gathered before him:

May I, on behalf of the whole community, offer to them our heartfelt sympathy, our reverent gratitude for the sacrifices which they were called upon to make, and may I tell them that in erecting this monument, we are not unmindful of their sorrows but that we are erecting it as a sign to this generation and to future generations with the high honour and esteem with which we regard those so dear to them, who gave all, who lost all and yet who gained all.

He then unveiled the memorial with the words 'Let us ever remember with thanksgiving and all honour before God and man the gallant sons of Sevenoaks who laid down their lives for their country in the Great War'.

Lord Sackville addresses the crowds before unveiling the Sevenoaks War Memorial

The Sevenoaks War Memorial, bedecked by floral tributes at its unveiling in October 1920. Over £5,000 was raised by local people to pay for it

The memorial included the name of Adrian Maurice Bartholomew, who was included incorrectly. Having survived the war, serving first with the Royal West Kent Regiment and then with the Royal Army Medical Corps, Bartholomew lived until 1966 and ensured that his own name was removed from the memorial. His brother-in-law, John Tester, was remembered correctly on the memorial, as his nephews, Eric and Leslie Tester, would be after their deaths at the end of the Second World War.

The War Memorial outside the church of St Nicholas, inscribed with the names of the fallen parishioners, was unveiled in December 1920 with a crowd of several hundred in attendance. In his address, the Rector hoped that the memorial would serve as a reminder, especially to children. The official unveiling was carried out by four children of the men, Masters Richardson and Castleden and the two sisters Francis, who removed the Union Jack from the memorial and, with the crowd, observed a moment's silence.

Lord Sackville then addressed the gathering on behalf of the ex-servicemen, many of whom would, like him, have known the men memorialised. As the *Chronicle* reported:

He himself could well remember in Gallipoli standing beside the hastily dug grave of a

The St Nicholas War Memorial

Sevenoaks soldier. He therefore thought the cross a most significant thing to the soldiers. They had known the lives of the fallen, had seen them die and were there that day to do honour to their memory.

Colonel Rogers of Riverhill spoke at a service to dedicate the Weald memorial. The German ideal was that might was right, observed Rogers, and the English that right was stronger than might. The English ideal had proved the better.

The Bishop of Rochester led the service held for the war memorial at St Mary, Kippington, which was attended by a crowd estimated to be three to four hundred strong.

A memorial to the fallen of Riverhead was unveiled by Earl Amherst in December 1919. A plaque in memory of one of these men, Sergeant William Dickman of the Royal West Kent Regiment, had already been put in place at Riverhead School in October 1919. For 20 years Dickman had been a teacher at the school and was active in the local community, including as Captain of Holmesdale Football Club. Dickman's father had been a butler to the Amherst family at their Montreal Estate and so it was fitting that his memorial tablet was made of oak from the estate and unveiled by Earl Amherst.

Among those remembered were Lord Stanhope's brother, Richard Philip. Lord Hillingdon's heir, Charles Thomas Mills, had been killed at Loos. The war deaths of the heirs to the local great estates had a lasting effect on landowning and use in and around Sevenoaks as estates were sold and broken up.

The fallen were remembered in a number of ways.
St Nicholas school created a Roll of Honour for its former pupils

Hidden Casualties

The euphoria and relief that news of peace bought gradually subsided. Local life slowly resumed its old routine. Men returned to their former employment and often sought comfort in their old comrades through different social networks

The familiar sight of soldiers in khaki was replaced by former servicemen with obvious disabilities. Others had less obvious but no less serious injuries. Continued efforts were made by organisations like Toc H, and the Comrades of the Great War to continue some of the ties that had bound the men closely together in wartime. Fred Pearce and his brothers were members of Toc H, the Christian organisation that had its roots in Talbot House, set up by the Reverend 'Tubby' Clayton during the war at Poperinghe, Belgium. There, soldiers had been welcome and treated equally, regardless of rank. Members of Toc H endeavoured to promote reconciliation and ease the sufferings of others. Three of the Pearce brothers would eventually have their ashes interred at the movement's church at All Hallows by the Tower, in London.

Despite the efforts of such organisations, there was clear evidence of the suffering that some endured. Some, like William John Ritchie, a former private in the Middlesex Regiment who had lost his sight, used the skills that he learnt at St Dunstan's (which provided training for blind ex-serviceman in order that they could support themselves rather than relying on charity) making and repairing willow baskets. Ritchie advertised his services in the *Sevenoaks Chronicle* in the early 1920s.

Stephen Copper who continued to ride his motorbike after
losing his arm. He lived to celebrate his 80th birthday

Stephen Copper had enlisted in September 1914 and served with the Royal West Kent Regiment. He was shot in the left arm in March 1916, the wound being so severe that the arm was later amputated. Once he had recuperated he returned to his former employer, and despite his injury, drove a motorbike as a delivery man for Kipps the butchers at St John's. Stephen was no doubt affected by the loss of three of his brothers and his brother-in-law during the war. His sister Amelia's husband, Sergeant Thomas Garrett of the Royal Garrison Artillery, had died of natural causes late in September 1918 in Salonika, Greece. Amelia Garrett and the many other widowed women of Sevenoaks, who had often suffered other wartime bereavements, were left to raise their children. Others had to contend with a returned husband who was never the same again.

Some men found life after the war too much to bear and the local paper recorded their circumstances. In November 1919, the paper reported a shell shock victim at Tubs Hill Station one Tuesday evening. A young passenger failed to produce a ticket for his journey and could not answer when asked by staff where he had come from. The staff took him in and gave him some food:

While eating this he suddenly bent down, put his hand to his head, and commenced to moan as if afraid of being struck by something. Thinking that he had possibly had a blow on the head, one of the officials made as though to touch his head, but he started off again, saying 'Whizz, whizz'. The police had meantime been communicated with and the man was removed to the Union.

Others, unable to deal with their experiences, returned home changed men, with all the implications for their family. Rose Baldwin of Seal was granted a separation order against her husband Charles Adam Baldwin, in 1929. The couple had been married in 1918 and had two children, a boy of eleven and a girl aged eight. Mrs Baldwin stated that the marriage had been very happy until her husband had begun to drink to excess after the birth of her first child. Charles Baldwin lived off his pension, having suffered from shell shock and neurasthenia. Baldwin was a country lad of 18 and living in Ightham when he enlisted in 1912 with the Queen's (Royal West Surrey) Regiment. He left for Le Havre with 1st Battalion in August 1914 and was shot a few weeks later in the October. He was invalided home and stayed until the summer of 1916 when he returned to the front line. In the July he was recorded as suffering from shell shock. He was discharged from the army on the grounds of his neurasthenia in November 1917.

Post war, Baldwin was well known to the police for drinking, bad language and other behaviour. On receiving the court summons he had returned home and *'proceeded to sell the whole of the furniture, lock, stock, and barrel for £2, including much of his wife's furniture'*. His whereabouts at the time of the court hearing was unknown and the order of separation was given with Mrs Baldwin being awarded custody of their children and her husband ordered to pay maintenance. In 1935, when Baldwin was charged with yet another count of being drunk and disorderly, the *Sevenoaks Chronicle* noted that:

Baldwin alleged that his drunkenness was caused through the war. He was terribly knocked about through the war and suffered with his nerves.

Charles Baldwin was killed in a motor accident in 1939 when, as a cyclist, he was following the hounds. The inquest jury returned a verdict of accidental death. Baldwin's bicycle was in a very poor condition and there was uncertainty as to how much he had been drinking, although it had been asserted that he had only had a pint and a half before setting off.

The *Chronicle* carried reports of men who took their own lives unable to cope, others were able to carry on but their weakened constitution no doubt contributed to their early death.

Joseph Sutton had fought in the war with the Queen's (Royal West Surrey) Regiment. Two of his brothers, Dick, a rifleman with the King's Royal Rifle Corps, and Percy, a signalman on *HMS Lavender*, were killed and are remembered on the Sevenoaks War Memorial. Joseph sustained a fractured skull in April 1918 at Messines Ridge and was discharged from the army as medically unfit. His injuries required several operations and caused him to become epileptic. The news report of his death in the *Sevenoaks Chronicle* stated that he had remained as cheerful as he could and was a much respected member of the Sevenoaks Services Club. He remained poorly for the rest of his life and died aged only 25 in 1924. He was buried in the churchyard at St Nicholas, Sevenoaks without any military ceremony.

Cecil George Thompson served for four years in France as a private with 76th Field Ambulance RASC and was recommended for the Military Medal. Both his older and younger brothers were killed during the war and are remembered on the town's memorial. Cecil had been demobilised in August 1919 before serving for six months with the Imperial War Graves Commission. In his obituary in the *Chronicle* in 1925, the paper linked Cecil's death with his war service. He had been blown up in a car in 1917 and suffered acutely from shell shock as a consequence.

> *Some five or six years ago the trouble reasserted itself, and he has been in ill-health ever since, but he had not become seriously ill till the day before his death, when he suddenly lapsed into unconsciousness.*

The paper noted that the date of Cecil's death – 25th September – had a number of associations for the family. Cecil had first crossed to France on September 25th 1915; his brother Sidney, serving with 7th Battalion City of London Regiment, was killed on 25th September 1916; his older brother, Captain Arthur Herbert Thompson of the King's Own Yorkshire Light Infantry, was killed on 25th September 1917. The family, sons of Arthur Thompson, former Superintendent of Sevenoaks Post Office was well known in Sevenoaks and news of Cecil's death, and full military funeral at Greatness Cemetery, was fully reported and no doubt keenly felt throughout the town. *'We are grateful'* wrote Arthur Thompson *'to all our Sevenoaks friends who have shown us such kindness in the loss of the last of our three soldier sons, we say from the bottom of our hearts – thank you.'*

In 1940, the *Sevenoaks Chronicle* reported the case of Albert Edward Chew. Chew, then aged 58, was found drunk, singing and shouting in the High Street, after drinking a toxic mix of beer and methylated spirit. Brought before the local magistrates he declared himself *'Guilty, sir, and I am very, very sorry'*. It was stated that Chew had tried hard to get work and did not normally drink methylated spirt, given to him on that occasion by another man. He had fallen on hard times and had already pawned his medals for 7s. He was able to provide the paperwork to demonstrate that he had kept up the payments in the hope of being able to recover his medals. The case was dismissed as a first offence on the understanding that Chew would leave the district.

This was not Chew's first appearance on such a charge. Before a previous court he had explained that:

> *He was hit on the head during the war and not been right since.*

Among his medals was the Distinguished Conduct Medal (DCM), which he had been awarded (*London Gazette*, 16th May 1916) as Gunner A E Chew of the 308th Trench Mortar Battery, Royal Field Artillery for:

> *Conspicuous gallantry when in charge of an isolated trench mortar gun. When his wires were cut he continued firing with good effect and observing for himself under very heavy fire.*

Chew's story clearly moved the magistrates who heard the case. One of their number, Sir Edward Meyerstein, paid the costs to redeem his medals and returned them to him.

Sevenoaks resident, Earl Beresford Moyce (born 1892) survived the Great War but was killed by the Germans nearly 30 years later. He had joined the Royal Navy in 1910 and served during the war on ships including the *Africa* and *Pembroke I*. He was demobilised in 1919 and returned to Sevenoaks where he lived with his wife, Edith née Sharrad. The couple lived at 42, Wickenden Road, Sevenoaks. It was here that they were killed on the night of 3rd March by a V2, along with seven other neighbours.

Fifty Years On – Veterans Return

Half a century ago, the 50th anniversary of the First World War prompted many veterans to remember their wartime service or to recall life at home during the conflict. Fortunately, some of these memories have been preserved as the *Sevenoaks Chronicle* reported the thoughts of these men as they either returned to Sevenoaks or looked back to their boyhoods to a time when thousands of soldiers were stationed in the town, along with many wounded at the local VAD hospitals, as well as the refugees from Belgium.

Fifty years after he had been stationed in Sevenoaks as a private with 5th Battalion King's Own Royal Lancaster Regiment, between November 1914 and February 1915, Harry Barrow returned to the town. Harry was interviewed by the *Sevenoaks Chronicle* during his visit and said:

Sevenoaks was utterly familiar. I booked into the famous Royal Oak Hotel and it had many of its 1914 qualities. Sevenoaks was still full of riches and Granville Road was no exception. At the junction with Eardley Road, recognisable to me at once, were the two detached houses commandeered for our battalion HQ and Quartermaster stores. Down at Tubs Hill, to my delight, I found the Elite. This was the local flea pit, a small music hall. On Thursday nights the local talent tried out its stuff. Entrance was 2d for men in uniform. The stage was still there but the laughing legion of the 5th King's Own had long since dissolved. On the other side of Tubs Hill station I found Holyoake Terrace and to reach it I drove over the main bridge where we had assembled on the bleak, historic, wet and cold St Valentine's Day 1915 to embark for France. At Knole Park, all I could do was peer in the gates and see again in flashback our battalion in trench digging practice. Little did I know that within a few months this was to become a stern reality.

In 1914 the main shopping street was full of dignified horse and carriage trade and urbanity. Now much of that personality was lost. The Shambles area retained its antiquity and I was delighted to find the pavilion band stand on the Vine had not changed. I was swept back to a Sunday afternoon where we sat expectantly in the gardens, a great concourse of khaki figures, when a lady mounted the platform. She wore a flimsy hat and, to our delight, Lancastrian red roses on her bosom. In a moment she slipped into the rousing, emotionally, recruiting song that was sweeping the country. A thousand cheers, a thousand pair of clapping hands, a thousand hearts wishing she would do the kissing now. And then her encore, 'You made me love you, I didn't want to do it'. She was Mrs Reubens, someone said, the wife of Paul Reubens, the composer.

John Edward Smith was featured in the *Sevenoaks Chronicle* in 1966 in his workshop at the foot of Wickenden Road. A gunmaker during the war, he was also best man at the wedding of the parents of future Prime Minister, Edward Heath. Smith worked at Woolwich Arsenal during the war, where he was in charge of a giant steam hammer, which could be adjusted so closely that it would come down on a watch placed on the anvil without breaking the glass. *'I used to do it regularly. When the hammer fell, you couldn't pull the watch out, but the glass was still intact'.*

Smith bored 100ft long gun barrels for naval vessels. When the Zeppelin raids came he would climb into a barrel and wait until the bombing as over. *'There was never a safer air raid shelter'.* He recalled seeing Zeppelins brought down at Potters Bar, Cuffley and Billericay and was close by when the Silvertown chemical works blew up.

Frederick Charles Zealey returned to Sevenoaks from further afield, having emigrated to Australia in 1920. Zealey was born in 1904 at the *Limes*, St John's, Sevenoaks, where his father was a well-known builder. He attended Cobden Road School before graduating to the school at nearby Bayham Road. Although too young to enlist himself, his brother, William John Zealey (1894–1960) served as a corporal with the West Kent Yeomanry and was stationed in India. Frederick recalled his memories of wartime Sevenoaks, writing for the *Sevenoaks Chronicle* that:

> I can remember when the firm of Quinnells, the removalists and contractors had a traction engine which pulled vans and wagons through the town, in 1911 – the Coronation year.
>
> This engine and three open wagons, all covered in bunting took all the school children up through the town to Knole Castle (sic) where we had a picnic on the green in front of the castle.
>
> I also remember Mr H Hill, the baker at St John's, with his bread cart and blind white pony – also Mr Kipps, the butcher, with his butcher's carts and his piebald pony Tetratch. It used to pull a governess cart or trap around the town, and in it would be Mr and Mrs Kipps, their daughter, and son George, who was killed in World War One.

Zealey continued:

> I have a photo of the men of the Royal West Kent Regiment on the Tubs Hill Station, waiting for the train to France on about 4th August, 1914. Sevenoaks in those days became a garrison town for troops, and many were in billets and empty houses. Regiments such as the Loyal North Lancashires, Yorkshires, and King's Own were stationed in Sevenoaks. I attended the unveiling of the War Memorial at the Vine after the war.
>
> The old cinema was opened before World War One and the prices listed in the Sevenoaks Courier were listed as two-pence a seat for children and nice plush seats for 6d and 9d and 1s for the gallery. There used to be a pianist to play and sometimes a violinist. You could hear us roar the house down at Charlie Chaplin, Steve Hart, Broncho Bill, John Bunny, and Flo Finch, and other old time film actors.
>
> We used to play in the old Oast House or hop kiln opposite the cinema, long since pulled down.

A Hundred Years On

Sevenoaks marked the centenary of the conflict in a number of ways. In August 2014, on the anniversary of the declaration of war, a special service was held at the Vine Memorial, attended by many descendants of the local men who had given their lives. Some relatives were also present at a candlelight vigil at Westminster Abbey to mark the start of the Great War centenary. Several families have since gone to extra lengths to remember their relatives, with some making the journey to their forbear's grave in one of the many Commonwealth War Grave cemeteries.

Descendants of many of the men named on the memorial
gathered to remember them in August 2014

Tim Marshall and his sons travelled to the grave of his great uncle, George Marshall, in 2017, also visiting the grave of Arnold Jarvis, George's boyhood friend with whom he emigrated

Tim Marshall with his sons at the grave of his Great Uncle, George Marshall, killed in 1917

Jack and Tom Larsson at the grave of Reverend Basil Plumptre MC

to Australia in 1912. Arnold's niece Tina Higgs and her husband have likewise visited both cemeteries. Tom Larsson and his brother Jack, not having close relatives of their own who fought, decided to research some of the men on the Sevenoaks War Memorial and visited a number of First World War sites, including the grave of Reverend Basil Plumptre MC.

In 2014, Abbie McGowan and Nicole Mounsey of Combe Bank School visited Cologne as part of a school trip and made a short film in memory of Private Horace Checkley, who died in 1918 of pneumonia, while a Prisoner of War, aged 19.

**Private Horace Henry Checkley, 1/6th Battalion
Northumberland Fusiliers**

The film, which had as its theme the homecoming that Horace never got to enjoy, was broadcast by BBC South East News and was seen by Horace's Great Nephew, David Checkley, who met the girls at their school to tell them more about Horace and his family, who lived on Golding Road.

Acts of remembrance like these ensure that the men and women of Sevenoaks, who lived and served through such a tumultuous period of history, are not forgotten.

BIBLIOGRAPHY

Gordon Anckorn (1979), *A Sevenoaks Camera* (Ashgrove Press: Sevenoaks)

Captain CT Atkinson (1924), *The Queen's Own Royal West Kent Regiment 1914-1918* (Pen & Sword reprint)

De Ruvigny, The Marquis, *The Roll of Honour, 1914-1918* (Naval & Military Press, reprint)

Peter Doyle (2016), *Kitchener's Mob: The New Army to the Somme* (The History Press)

John Dunlop (1964), *The Pleasant Town of Sevenoaks* (Caxton and Holmesdale Press: Sevenoaks)

Jean Fox et al (2007), *Seal, the Story of a Parish* (Phillimore & Co. Hampshire)

David Killingray & Elizabeth Purves (2012), *Sevenoaks, An historical dictionary* (Phillimore & Co. Hampshire)

Bob Ogley & Roger Perkins (1999), *Sevenoaks Chronicle of the Century* (Froglets Publications: Westerham)

Reverend John Rooker, *A History of the War for Children* (privately published)

Vita Sackville-West (1937), *Pepita* (Hogarth Press: London)

Peter Simkins (2007), *Kitchener's Army* (Pen & Sword)

Charles Stanhope (2006), *The War Memoirs of Earl Stanhope of Chevening* (Tom Donovan editions)

Henry Williamson (1955), *A Fox Under My Cloak* (Macdonald: London)

Illustration Sources

Unless otherwise stated, all images are in the personal collection of the author. Every attempt has been made to acknowledge copyright for each image. My thanks to the following for permission to reproduce images on the relevant pages:

Page 16, the Horncastle family; page 22 the family of Leslie Mattholi; page 32 (and cover photo) photo of Albert Kent courtesy of Barbara and Keith Reddy; Page 34 image of Fred-

～

ABOUT THE AUTHOR

Matthew Ball is a historian, genealogist and author. He moved to Sevenoaks in 2008 and has spent over five years chronicling the impact of the First World War on the town. He is particularly interested in the Queen's Own Royal West Kent Regiment.